LIEUT. MACPHERSON'S REPORT UPON THE KHONDS OF THE DISTRICTS OF GANJAM AND CUTTACK

LIEUT. MACPHERSON'S REPORT

UPON

THE KHONDS

OF

THE DISTRICTS

OF

GANJAM AND CUTTACK.

BY

SAMUEL CHARTERS MACPHERSON

GYAN

Published by

Gyan Publishing House
5, Ansari Road
Daryaganj, New Delhi-110002
Phone: 011-47034999, 9811692060
E-mail: books@gyanbooks.com

Distribution Network
gyanbooks.com
India, USA, Canada, UK, Australia

ISBN: 978-81-212-2042-2 (PB)
First Published, 1842

2nd Impression 2024

Printed at: Gyan Press, Delhi.

LIEUT. MACPHERSON'S REPORT UPON THE KHONDS OF THE DISTRICTS OF GANJAM AND CUTTACK
Author: SAMUEL CHARTERS MACPHERSON

LIEUT. MACPHERSON'S

Report

UPON

THE KHONDS

OF

THE DISTRICTS

OF

GANJAM AND CUTTACK.

CALCUTTA:

G. H. HUTTMANN, BENGAL MILITARY ORPHAN PRESS.

1842.

To the Chief Secretary to Government,

FORT ST. GEORGE.

SIR,

With reference to the Extract from the Minutes of Consultation by the Right Honorable the Governor in Council, in the Revenue Department, under date the 27th February 1841, which was communicated to me, I have the honor to forward to you a Report upon the Khoonds of the Districts of Ganjam and Cuttack, with an included Map and an Appendix.

I shall have the honor on a future occasion to submit the results of my enquiries respecting the "Sourah" race, the only other Hill people of Orissa, with respect to which I possess any information.

(Signed) S. C. MACPHERSON, *Lieut.*,
Asst. Surveyor General.

MADRAS,
21*st June*, 1841.

(A true Copy,)

HY. CHAMIER,
Chief Secretary.

CONTENTS,

THE PLAN OF THIS REPORT, AND THE SOURCES OF THE INFORMATION UPON WHICH IT IS FOUNDED.

PART I.

OF THE RELATION OF THE KHOND POPULATION OF THE ZEMINDARIES OF GOOMSUR AND BOAD TO THE HINDU PEOPLE.

SECTION I.

INTRODUCTION.

SECTION II.

OF THE RELATIONS OF THE KHOND POPULATION OF GOOMSUR TO THAT ZEMINDARY.

SECTION III.

RELATION OF THE KHOND POPULATION OF BOAD TO THAT ZEMINDARY.

Its relation to the Khond Tribes identical in its foundation, but different in its practical spirit from that which exists between Goomsur and its Hill Tribes, and owing to the influence of two general causes—The mode in which Military aid is rendered by the Khonds to the Zemindars—Forms similar to those of "Homage" and "Investiture"—Maliah Khonds confer dress of investiture on Zemindar.

PART II.

OF THE USAGES OF THE MOUNTAIN TRIBES RELATING TO THE GOVERNMENT OF SOCIETY.

SECTION I.

OF THE DIVISIONS OF SOCIETY AND OF THE PATRIARCHAL AUTHORITY AMONGST THE KHONDS.

The system of Khond Society Patriarchal—Tribes and their Subdivisions, with their Patriarchs—Federal Groups—Councils of Tribes and Subdivisions and of Groups—Of the Government of a Tribe—The basis of the Patriarchal authority—Partly founded upon birth, partly upon choice, partly upon religious feeling—The nature and the duties of the Patriarchal Office—Abbaya of a Subdivision—Abbaya of a Village—Descent of the Patriarchal Office—In case of non-age—Recognition of a Patriarch on his accession to Office.

SECTION II.

THE PUBLIC ASSEMBLIES OF THE KHOND TRIBES.

The public Councils of a Khond Tribe—Arrangement—Manner of discussion—Councils of Subdivisions and of Villages.

SECTION III.

OF THE CONFEDERATIONS OF THE KHOND TRIBES IN GOOMSUR AND BOAD.

The basis of these unions—Each Group presided over by a chief Patriarch, who is also the Agent of the Zemindar for Khond affairs—Duties of the federal head of a Group as Agent of the Zemindar—The Dora Bissye of Goomsur—The Khonro of Boad—Federal Councils.

SECTION IV.

FAMILY OF THE KHONRO OF BOAD AND DORA BISSYE OF GOOMSUR.

1.—*Family of the Khonro of Boad.*

Its Traditions broken—Four brothers of the Doobakkia family came from the Zemindary of Kunjeur—The youngest brother head of the house—The third brother a Priest—The second brother a Naick—The elder brother a Messenger.

2.—*Family of the Dora Bissye of Goomsur.*

Its primitive seats—Its Head resided at Koladah, compelled to retire to possessions under the Ghauts—Assumed designation of "Raj Benniahs"—The distinction of "Dora" when acquired.

SECTION V.

HEREDITARY HINDU OFFICERS OF THE TRIBES OF BOAD.

Origin of this class of employes—Designations—In what Districts—Caste—Doogalos of Goomsur Duties—Rank—The case of the Mahalicko of Nowsagur—That of the Bissye of Hodzoghoro.

PART III.

OF THE USAGES OF INTERCOURSE OF THE KHOND TRIBES.

These Tribes have no idea of public rights or duties apart from express compacts—Ideas of duty towards our Government—Towards the Zemindaries in which they are included—Peace is their prevailing condition—Origin and course of a Khond feud—That between portions of the Athara Mootah, and Burra Des in Goomsur—That between Bulscoopa and Dommosinghi—Khond contests intermitted.

PART IV.

OF USAGE IN THE PLACE OF CIVIL LAWS.

1.—*Of Offences against the person.*

Murder, Homicide, Manslaughter and Wounding.

2.—*Of Offences against Property.*

Theft—Wrongful occupation of the Soil.

3.—*Of Adultery.*

Adultery where established by the testimony of the husband.

4.—*Law of Inheritance.*

Of Landed Property and Agricultural Stock—Moveables—In case of failure of heirs.

5.—*Law of Property in Land.*

Land possessed without Tenure—Waste Land.

6.—Rules relative to the transference of Land by sale.

7.—Procedure of Judicial Councils.

Procedure in deciding questions of property in land, and the greater offences against the person. Enquiry by testimony on oath and by ordeal costs of suit.

PART V.

Of the Manners of the Mountain Khonds.

SECTION I.

Of the Paternal Authority amongst the Khonds, their Industry.

The strength of the paternal authority—System of Family life—Sons cannot possess property before their Fathers' death—Practise agriculture alone—Hindu castes settled on the hills—Manner of labor—Rich in agriculture stock—Hill produce—Market value of land—Mode of exchange.

SECTION II.

Other Elements in the character of the Khonds.

Universal hospitality—Meriahs and Guests—Involuntary guests—A tribe guests—Love of personal independence—Attachment to persons not to institutions —Fidelity and public engagements—Endurance of physical suffering—Some districts Chiefs read and write—Nowbhun Khonro—Dora Bissye.

SECTION III.

Of the relations of the Sexes and Domestic Ceremonies.

Influence of Women—Regarded with respect—who can marry—The Wife older than the Husband—The Wife not the property of the Husband—Polygamy and Concubinage—Observance of marriage tie—Drunkenness—Disgraceful—Births —Deaths.

SECTION IV.

Usages of War—Convivial Habits—Habitations—Dress—Medicines—Language.

Physical character—Sacrifice and Dress before Battle—Arms—Character of Feasts—Clothing—Habitations.

PART VI.

Of the Religion of the Khonds.

SECTION I.

Of the Doctrines of the Khond Religion.

Fundamental ideas of the Khond superstition analogous to those of other races at a similar stage of mental advancement. Two classes of Native divinities. One Hindu divinity.

Of the Khond Divinities generally acknowledged.

1.—*Beera Pennoo, or the Earth God, in Orissan Bhoomi Devita.*

Beera Pennoo, or the Earth God, worshipped under two characters—Attributes of his comprehensive character—Attributes as the divinity presiding over the powers of nature—Institution of the rite of human sacrifice—Occasions of sacrifice—Public sacrifices, each crop requires blood—Private sacrifices—Number of victims—The victims how procured—Acceptable victims must be brought—occasionally married—condition of the children of victims—Father and child not sacrificed in the same district—Escape of a victim—The rite lasts three days—The Meria grove and stream—The place of sacrifice—The sacrifice.

2.—Bella Pennoo, the Sun God, and Dauzoo Pennoo, the Moon God.

3.—Sundi Pennoo, the God of Limits, adored by human victims on boundaries—other victims.

4.—Loha Pennoo, the God of Arms—His symbol—When invoked victims.

5.—Joogah Pennoo, the God of Small Pox—His offerings.

6.—Nadzoo Pennoo, the Village God—His functions—Victims and Priests.

7.—Soro Pennoo, the Hill God, Jori Pennoo, the God of Streams, and "Gossa Pennoo," the Forest God.

8.—"Moonda Pennoo," the Tank God.

9.—"Soogoo Pennoo," or Sidroojoo Pennoo, the God of Fountains.

10.—Pidzoo Pennoo, the God of Rain.

11.—Pilamoo Pennoo, the God of Hunting.

12.—God of Births.—The Khond local Divinities.

2.—Peetabuldee—The Great Father God—His name—where worshipped—His shrines—His offerings.

3.—Bandri Penno—His shrines appeared in a material form at Borapal—effects of his removal.

4.—Bahmun Pennoo and Bahmoondi Pennoo.

5.—Dhoongurri Pennoo. His worship.

6.—Singa Pennoo.—Singa Pennoo manifested in Oogdoor, stolen—His nature.

7.—Dommosinghiani.

8.—Potterghor.

9.—Pinjai.
10.—Bulinda Silenda.
11.—Kunkali.

Dommosinghiani tutelary God of Dommosinghi, "Potterghor" and Purjai, names of places; Bulinda Silenda, and Kunkali.

THE HINDU GODDESS KALI.

SECTION II.

THE KHOND PRIESTHOOD.

Origin of its two classes.—1. The Khond priesthood—Appellations—In what respect separated from the community—Magical Arts—Equality—Emoluments.—2. Hindu priests.

SECTION III.

Of the influence which the religion of the Khonds exerts upon society.

PART VII.

Of measures to be adopted towards the Mountain Khonds.

SECTION I.

The history of our connection with the Khoonds—Our objects with respect to them.

SECTION II.

Of measures to be adopted with reference to the religion of the Khonds.

SECTION III.

The Khonds, South of the Mahanuddee, should be included in one plan of operations.

SECTION IV.

What relations we shall establish with the Khond Tribes as subjects.

SECTION V.

Of the mode of introducing our authority amongst the Khond Tribes.

SECTION VI.

Of measures more especially directed to the abolition of the rite of human sacrifice.

SECTION VII.

Of legal provisions for the punishment of the offence of traffic in human victims.

SECTION VIII.

Of Roads and Fairs in the Khond Country.

SECTION IX.

Of the Agency required for the execution of these measures.

CONTENTS OF APPENDIX.

NOTE I.

1.—Analysis of Population in the Town of Boad, including all the Castes in the Zemindary.

NOTE II.

2.—Chief Vegetable products of the Zemindaries of Goomsur and Boad, and of their connected Khond Districts above and below the Ghauts.

NOTE III.

3.—Hindu Castes of the North Eastern Districts of Goomsur.

NOTE IV.

4.—The Geological features of a portion of Goomsur aud Boad.

NOTE V.

5.—Minor Subdivisions of the Khonds—Statistical Statements of which a Synoptical view has been given respecting—

6.—The Khalisah of Boad.

7.—The thirteen Khond Districts in Boad.

8.—The Khond Districts formerly attached to Boad now to Goomsur.

9.—The Khond District attached to Duspullah.

The Plan of this paper; and the sources of the information upon which it is founded.

It is my purpose in the following paper, to describe the portion of the Khond people, which I have observed in the districts of Ganjam and Cuttack, and principally in the Zemindaries of Boad, Goomsur, and Duspullah; and to state my views as to the measures which should be adopted towards them.

I shall endeavour, 1st, to state the relations, which the Khond population of those districts bears to the Hindu people.

2dly. I shall describe their usages, whether relating to the Government of society, or to intercourse between Tribes, or as they appear in the place of Civil Laws.

3dly. I shall describe their Manners.

4thly. I shall give an account of their Religion.

I shall then state the principles of the measures, which in my judgment should be adopted towards them,—1st, as question of policy,—2dly, with a view to the abolition of the sanguinary rites of their Religion.

The information which is here submitted to the Government, was obtained during my employment with my Regiment, and on survey under the orders of the Commissioner in Goomsur and Sourahdah, during the years 1836 and 1837; and the following year, from intercourse with Dora Bissye, the Chief Khond Patriarch of Goomsur, and with other prisoners of Ganjam.

The effects of exposure in the most unhealthy parts of the region of the Ghauts then compelled me to leave India for two years, and it has only now become possible for me to attempt to exhibit the results of my enquiries.

Those results and the practical measures which they appear to me to indicate, I offer for the consideration of the Government, in compliance with its orders with extreme diffidence. But I conceive that in the present state of our knowledge, no attempt to elucidate the character and social condition of this new people, or to devise means for the accomplishment of the objects, which our relative situation imposes upon us may be deemed presumptuous.

I confide that in any event the imperfections of a work of considerable labor, executed under the circumstances adverted to, will be regarded by the Government with indulgence.

The chief sources of my informations have been the following:

1. The Bansovulli or Book of Family Records of Goomsur.
2. The Bansovulli of Boad.

3. The Rajah of Boad and his principal servants.

4. Nowbhun Khouro, the Chief Khond Patriarch of Boad, who met me in the district of Atcombo.

5. Madhwa Khouro, the present " Khouro," whom I saw in the same district.

6. Myser Mullick, Chief Patriarch of Ruttabarri, whom I visited there.

7. Dammo Jenni, one of the two chief Patriarchs of Borogootza, whom I met there.

8. Poora Bissye, and the Patriarch Cundo Mulliko of Bulscoopa, whom I met there.

9. Nittar Naick and the chief Patriarch Ghussi Mulliko of Dummosinghi, who came from thence to Courminghia to meet me.

10. Babano Mullicko, Chief Patriarch of Oogdoor, who met me at Boad.

11. Bagwan Son, Chief Patriarch of Bara Mullick, who met me at Boad.

12. A Nephew of the Chief Patriarch of Punchora, who came to meet at Boad.

13. Sam Bissye at Hodgzoghoro.

14. Ootan Sing Dulbehra whom I saw at Tentilghoro.

15. The Hindu Collector of Tolls at Gattigooda, and other Hindus whom I found in Chokapaud.

16, The Chief Patriarch Oosera Majee whom I visited in Nowsagur in the Duspullah Zemindarry.

17. The Chief Patriarch of Goomsur, Dora Bissye, when in confinement at Ganjam.

18. The Cazzis and Curnums of several of the Districts of Goomsur below the Ghauts.

19. Khond and Hindu prisoners in the jail at Ganjam.

PART I.

Of the relation of the Khond Population of the Zemindaries of Goomsur and Boad, to the Hindu People.

SECTION I.

Introduction.

Natural and Political Divisions of Orissa—Maritime Division, Subalpine Division, Alpine Division—Three principal primitive races, the Koles, Khonds and Sourahs—Region of the Khond Race—Region of the Sourah Race—These observations relate chiefly to the Khonds of the Zemindaries of Goomsur and Boad—Limits, and Geographical situation of the Zemindary of Boad. Of that of Goomsur—Synopsis of Statistical Facts relative to these, and to their connected Khond Districts—The general situation of the Khonds as an aboriginal people of India—We first came into immediate contact with them in 1835—Their gradual expulsion from their ancient Territories by the Hindus—Their names.

1. The light of authentic history dawns upon the ancient Kingdom of Orissa at the period of the accession of the Kesari dynasty to its throne, A. D. 473, and in Natural and Political Divisions of Orissa.

the ninth century plainly discloses its great social features, which then bore the analogy to its geographical divisions which still exists between them.

Asiat. Trans. Vol. XVI.

2. The Territory of Orissa, when the power of the Gajapati Sovereigns was at its zenith, occupied a space measuring six degrees in latitude, between the valley of the Ganges and that of the Godavery, and having a mean breadth of about three degrees in longitude. It was traversed in its whole length by the range of Eastern Ghauts, running at an average distance of seventy miles from the Coast of Coromandel, and was naturally divided, by no strong lines of demarcation, into an Alpine, a Subalpine, and a Maritime Region.

Maritime Division.

3. 1st.—Its Maritime Division extended along the whole Sea board, with an average breadth of fifteen miles. It was an open, salubrious, and highly productive expanse, with the exception of a tract of marshy and forest-covered deltas, intersected by lagunes, which was situated in its Northern portion. The open and fertile parts of this Territory formed, in conformity with the general usage, the Khalisah or State Domain, whilst the wilder and less accessible Districts were partitioned into a number of Zemindaries of very various rank, value, and extent.

Subalpine Division.

4. 2d.—The Subalpine Region comprehended the subordinate ramifications, and the dependent hill groups of the great mountain chain upon either side, with the extensive tracts of country which they embraced. It comprized above one half of the entire area of the kingdom, forming a vast, ill-explored, expanse of hilly wastes, impenetrable forests, and swampy wood-lands, interspersed with numerous vallies generally characterized by beauty and fertility, and broken occasionally by broad and productive plains.

5. This Region was divided into a large number of Zemindaries, some of which bearing the rank of petty Principalities—have made a considerable figure in the history of the Eastern Division of the Peninsula of India.

6. The subject of the relation of these great Estates to the Orissan Monarchy, and to the Empires in which they have been included since its fall, has been obscured rather than illustrated by the application to it of the terms and analogies of feudalism, by writers who have regarded its objects, and its external features, rather than its origin, its principles, and its spirit.

7. These Zemindary Domains vary in point of extent, from inconsiderable Estates of small value, to Territories of great dimensions, yielding large Revenues. The latter are possessed by families which derive their origin from the Royal Houses of Orissa, or from the principal stocks of Rajpootana, or which have sprung from successful adventurers generally of two classes, the leaders of predatory bands, and great provincial officers, in whose hands administrative have passed into proprietary rights.

8. But the greater Zemindars of Orissa as a body, do not owe their Territories like the original nobility of feudal Europe, to the direct patronage of a Sovereign,

nor their authority to the social wants of a particular age. Their possessions were generally acquired by the enterprize or by the policy of the founders of each house; either conquered from earlier Hindu proprietors, or wrested from the primitive occupants of the soil, or severed by fraud and force from the State. But all have acknowledged the theoretical supremacy, in succession of the Orissan Monarchy, of that of Delhi, of the Mahratta power, and of our empire, accepting from each either original or renewed Deeds of Tenure, which bear every date within a period of twelve centuries, and exemplify conditions endlessly varied.

9. The precarious and unfruitful allegiance which they have yielded to these powers has been signified by the payment of Tribute, which under our rule, is, in some quarters nominal, in some heavy; by the performance of services generally formal, and the maintenance of nominal Contingents.

10. But the Chiefs of these Estates have always borne the title of Rajah, and have generally exercised, with few practical limitations, all the powers of independent Sovereignty, ruling the haughty and uncontrolled despots of their wild domains—save where revolts have arisen, generally from the operation of unsuitable laws and excessive assessments, and we have bent them completely or partially to our yoke.

Alpine Division.

11. 3d. The Alpine Region, comprising the central ridges, the lofty plateau, and the inner vallies of the chain of Ghauts, with the great tracts of forest by which they are surrounded, has been occupied from the earliest historical period, as it is at present, chiefly by remnants of three races which claim, with the universal support of tradition, the aboriginal possession not of this portion alone, but of the greater part of the soil of Orissa.

Three primitive races.

12. Of these remnants, the Koles prevail in the northern parts, the Khonds in the middle region, and the Sourahs in the south; and whilst each of these holds exclusive possession of a part of the central tracts of mountain and forest, it exists also, thinly scattered over portions of the Zemindary domains, under various relations to the Hindu people.

Region of the Khond race.

13. The Khonds are now seen, in both of these situations, within the following ill defined limits. Upon the east they appear scattered over the wilder tracts of the Ganjam district bordering upon the Chilka Lake, and are seen in that quarter at a few points, upon the coast of the Bay of Bengal. They are found, on the north-west, on the confines of Gondwana, in longitude 83°, while on the west, they extend within the unsurveyed frontier of Berar. They are found as far south as Bustur in latitude 19° 40′, while the Zemindary of Palconda is like that of Kunnapoor possessed by a Khond Chief on the south-east, they are replaced on the limits of the Souradah and Moherry districts in Ganjam, by the Sourah race, which thenceforward occupies the eastern acclivities of the Ghauts to the Godavery. To the north, fifty miles beyond the Mahanuddee, in the meridian of Boad, they are succeeded by the Kole people on the north east, they are found high in Cuttack, while Sourahs (not identified with the southern race) there inhabit the inferior ridges of the Ghauts.

14. The extreme length of the territory which is thus indicated, is about two hundred, its extreme breadth about one hundred and seventy miles ; and it is unequally divided by the Mahanuddee flowing from west to east in 20° 40′ N. lat.

Region of the Sourah race.

15. The Sourah race extends from the Kimedy Zemindary which adjoins Goomsur upon the south to the Godavery, a region two hundred miles in length, which is almost entirely unexplored.

Division of the Khonds to which these observations relate is included in Goomsur and Boad.

16. I propose to present an outline of the system of social and individual life of the portion of the Khond people, which has fallen under my observation, to the south of the Mahanuddee; and principally in the Zemindaries of Boad and Goomsur; two Domains which hold a high rank amongst the great Estate of Orissa, whether in respect of extent, of antiquity, or of the dignity of the families by which they havê been possessed.

17. With respect to the unobserved Sourah race it is in my power to offer only a brief and imperfect sketch of its system of superstition, which is distinctly identical in its foundation with that of the Khonds, rendering this people necessarily an object of the same class of practical measures. A brief notice of the leading geographical features of each of the Domains of Boad and Goomsur, and of the Khond Districts, which are included in them, and a synoptical view of the few statistical facts which have been ascertained relative to them, will complete these introductory observations.

Situation and Geographical features of Boad.

18. I. The Zemindary of Boad, at the middle of the last century, extended between the lines of 20° and 21° 20′ N. L. and those of 83° 40′ and 84° 5′ East longitude, comprising an area of about 3,500 square miles.

19. The Mahanuddee, breaking in a majestic stream through the eastern chain of Ghauts, divided it into two unequal portions, above a third part lying upon its northern, the remainder along its southern bank. The division situated to the north of the River, now constitutes the distinct Estate of Autmullick, and Boad is, therefore, at present bounded, upon the north, by the great river, on the west by the Tale Nuddee, which divides it from the Patera Zemindary ; on the east by the Kolkola Rivulet, by which it is parted from that of Duspullah ; and on the south by Goomsur, and its area is estimated at 1,900 square miles.

20. The territory of Boad as thus defined, is situated entirely in the hydrographical valley of the Mahanuddee, and is composed of two distinct portions, 1st, an alluvial plain of irregular breadth, which lies between the southern bank of the river and the bases of the divided chain of Ghauts; and 2dly, a part of the great mountain range, the central ridge of which here expands into a broad and lofty plateau.

The Khalisah or Domain of Boad.

21. 1st.—The alluvial tract (with the exception of one or two sections) constitutes the Khalisah or Domain ; and is exclusively inhabited by Hindus of the classes which are enumerated below.* Its area is 500 square miles, of which,

* Vide Appendix, Note I.

probably, a fifth part is cultivated. The remainder is a wild expanse of hills, forests, water-courses, and stony wastes. The Khalisah of Boad is divided into nine Mootahs which contain 165 villages, of which the population is estimated at 6,000 souls. Its soil is of average fertility, according to the somewhat low standard of Orissa. The most important vegetable products both of the alluvial and alpine portions of this Zemindary, and of Goomsur, are enumerated elsewhere. Its climate, which in its general characters, is that of all Orissa, is considered less unhealthy than that of some of the other forest Zemindaries on the Mahanuddee. Note II.

22. 2d.—The portion of the region of the Ghauts, which is included in Boad, and in the contiguous Zemindary of Goomsur, is occupied exclusively by the Khond race. It is composed partly of the central table land which is here formed by the expansion of the spinal ridge of the mountain chain; partly of its numerous lateral ramifications which guide the drainage of its northern and north-western slopes to the Mahanuddee, through the domain of Boad, as the streams of its eastern acclivities water the Khalisah Goomsur on their way to the Russagaila River which reaches the Sea at Ganjam. The vast forest which extends uninterruptedly through Orissa, from the banks of the Godavery to those of the Ganges, a distance of nearly 600 miles, at this point completely envelopes in its umbrageous canopy the bases and the sides of the mountain chain; stretching without a visible limit to the north of Boad, over the successive ranges which rise beyond the river; and forming a zone from fifteen to thirty miles in depth along the eastern face of the Ghauts on the side of Goomsur. The mountain region of Boad and of Goomsur.

23. The central table lands bears the same general characters in both Zemindaries. It has an average elevation of about 2,000 feet. Its surface is divided into a few principal and numerous secondary vallies, which are generally open, simply connected, and of easy inclination, although parted by ridges of very various altitude. The great forest sends large off-shoots up the exterior vallies of the plateau which occasionally rise above its edges and meet from either side. But many considerable tracts are perfectly bare of wood; others are lightly sprinkled with the forest trees of luxuriant growth, scattered singly and in clumps, some portions are covered with light bushy jungle rich in flowers, while in some dark groves every where mark the abutments and deeper recesses of the hills. The climate of this region has been proved to be like that of every other forest-girt plateau in India of similar elevation, as highly insalubrious as that of the wooded districts below its soil, beneath the influence of never failing rains, and perennial springs, yields a rich return to the skilful and energetic industry of the Khonds.* Vide Note on the Geological features of Goomsur and Boad.

* Vide Note II.

24. Of the principal vallies which descend either from the table land, or from the ridge of Hydrographical partition which proceeds from it on either hand, that of the Bortungia River, which taking its rise on the edge of the plateau flows eastward through Chokapand, is fertile nearly throughout its whole course. The rivulet which passes by Raneegunge enriches tracts of some importance. The Salki which flows northward down the centre of the plateau, although a rapid, is a productive stream. The Bulwad and the Gohera are periodical rivulets of little value. The Bagh Nuddee and the Tale Nuddee enrich the country through which they pass.

The portion of this mountain region which is included in Boad, has an area of 1400 square miles, and it is divided into fifteen Khond Districts, the population of which is estimated at about 20,000 souls.

Situation and Geographical features of Goomsur.

25. II. The Zemindary of Goomsur is included within the lines of 19° 36′ 3″ and 20° 20′ North latitude and those of 84° 14′ and 85° 1′ East longitude, and has an area of 1,350 squares miles. On the northern and north-western sides, it is bounded by the Zemindaries of Duspullah and Boad; on the north-eastern and eastern by the Zemindary of Nyaghur; on the west it touches the Khond Districts of Boad and of Chinna Kimedy. On the south-west it is bounded by the Estates of Karadah, Runnabah and Souradah. Upon the south it meets the Moherry Zemindary and Daracottah, and upon the south-east the Zemindary of Autghur.

26. Goomsur, like Boad, is divided into an Alpine and a Subalpine portion, of which the former as above observed, is possessed by the Khonds, while the latter constitutes the Khalisah or Domain. It is divided into eighteen Mootahs which contain 464 villages. Its population, which is estimated at 61,000 souls, is exclusively Hindu,* except in a limited tract in its south-western angle,—and where families of the ancient people exist in hamlets thinly scattered amongst its least productive wilds.

* Vide Appendix Note III.

The Khalisah of Goomsur.

27. The area of the Domain is 840, that of the Khond Districts about 500 square miles. The former situated beneath the eastern face of the great mountain range, occupies the upper portion of the valley of the Russagorla, a considerable stream which rising from many widely spread sources amongst the Ghauts, reaches the sea at Ganjam by a winding course of about 150 miles. The western division of the Domain, lying immediately at the base of the mountain plateau, is principally composed of the narrow and rugged glens amongst which the feeders of this river rise. It is included within the great forest of Orissa, which is here interspersed with open glades of great beauty, and frequently varied by lightly wooded tracts in which, by the streams, villages flourish amongst rich corn fields, gardens and orchards. These glens becoming gradually less densely wooded, and less insalubrious as they recede from the mountains, expand into open and highly productive vallies upon the eastern frontier of the Zemindary; but of the whole Khalisah of Goomsur, little more than a fourth part is cultivated.

28. Of the Khond Districts of Goomsur, three are situated upon the plateau described above; the fourth lies within the forest at its base. Of the population of any save the latter District (Chokapaud) no estimate has been formed.

29. The following Statements exhibit the statistical facts relating, 1st, to the Khalisah of Boad, and 2dly, to its Khond Districts, which I have ascertained from the sources referred to in the Appendix.

30. The third Statement, relative to the Khalisah of Goomsur, is taken from Returns obtained from the office of the Collector of Ganjam by Lieutenant Hill.

I.

The Khalisah or Domain of Boad.

Mootahs.	*Villages.*	*Houses.*	*Peons.*	*Total Population.*	*Area.*
Koosunghur, including the Khond District of Kotrikia which contains 14 Villages, ...	24	270	211	1080	
Harbunga, ...	18	177	74	608	
Ramghur, ...	14	144	28	376	
Koradyhur, ...	11	88	0	352	
Machuchund, ...	55	481	128	1924	
Moodjeund, ...	22	222	165	888	
Byra Des with Soat Mullick, containing 146 Villages, ...	8	49	15	196	
The Fort of Poorna Cuttack, and Villages, ...	7	93	26	372	
The Fort of Bowerah and Villages, ...	6	30	15	120	
	165	1524	656	6096	500 Sq. Miles.

II.

THE KHOND DISTRICTS OF BOAD.

The fifteen Khond Districts of Boad, (with Hodzogoro now connected with Goomsur.)

Districts.	*Chiefs.*	*Mootahs.*	*Villages.*	*Houses.*	*Peons.*	*Population.*	*Area.*
Kotrikia, ...	Puttiah Mullicko, ...	4	14	112	...	560	
Eastern Atcombo, ...	Madhwa Khonro, ...	4	32	232	...	1165	
Western Atcombo, ...	Myser Mullicko, ...	4	30	240	...	1200	
Booroogootza, ...	Dammo Jenni and Pedda Debri, ...	3	28	389	...	1945	
Bulscoopa, ...	Cundo Mullicko and Poora Bissye	7	72	821	...	360	
Dommosinghi, ...	Ghassi Mullicko and Nittar Nackoo Soodoo, ...	3	16	175	...	80	
Oogdoor, ...	Babana Mullicko, ...	1	10	100	...	500	
Bagjeer, ...	Goda Mullicko, ...	1	11	88	...	440	
Bara Mullick, ...	Bagwan Sow, ...	1	23	184	..	920	
Kolabagh, ...	Durrai Mullicko, the Maha Mullicko Pondo Khonro Sundolo Mullicko, ...	3	12	96	...	480	
Bondoghur, ...	Bisskissun Bissye, ...	2	30	240	...	1200	
Punchora, ...	Rutto Mullicko, ...	13	232	1856	...	9280	
Saat Mullick, ...	Babino Mullicko, ...	1	14	112	...	560	
Hodzoghora, transferred to Goomsur, ...	Rabo Mullicko and Sani Bissye, ...	6	50	400	...	2000	
Tentiliaghor, ...	Rabo Mullicko and Ootan Sing Dulbehra, ...	6	47	400	..	1590	
	Total, ...	59	621	5446	...	22079	1400 Sq. Miles.

III.

GOOMSUR PROPER.

According to the Collector's Returns.

30. *Extracted from Lieutenant Hill's Survey Report on Goomsur.*

Mootahs.	*Villages.*	*Peons armed with Matchlocks.*	*Dandassies, &c. armed with Bows and Axes.*	*Pauns & Khonds similarly armed.*	*Total armed Population.*	*Remaining Population.*	*Total Population of Goomsur Proper.*	*Area of Goomsur Proper.*	*Cultivated area of Goomsur Proper.*
18	464	2524	342	810	3730	58136	61866	820 S. M.	200 M.

IV.

The Khond Districts of Goomsur.

Districts.	*Chiefs.*	*Mootahs.*	*Villages.*	*Houses.*	*Peons.*	*Population.*	*Area.*
Chokapaud, ...	Baghero Mullicko, Rugnath Bissye,	12	86	557	0	2285	
Athara Mootah,...	....	not accurately ascertained.					
Bara Mootah,......	....	not accurately ascertained.					
Hodzoghoro, ...	Rabo Mullicko, Sam Bissye,.......	given in Statement No. II.					

31. With respect to Table No. II, it is to be observed that I have retained amongst the Khond Districts of Boad, for reasons which will appear hereafter, the District or half District of Hodzoghoro which is now included in Goomsur, the average number of houses in the Hindu villages of Boad appears to be ten, that in the Khond hamlets eight. The number of inhabitants to a house I have in the former case assumed at four, in the latter at five.

32. It is to be observed that the Statement No. III, respecting Goomsur proper, gives upon the latter calculation the average of 30 houses to a village, Khond hamlets inclusive; a result which requires confirmation.

33. A reference to the Appendix will show how much of the above statements is founded upon exact returns, how much is estimated from the averages which those returns afford.

34. Such are the general observations by which it appears necessary to preface the description of the portion of the Khond population of the Zemindaries of Goomsur and Boad, which I have visited.

35. This race is obviously one of the numerous remnants of the primitive population of India, which have survived the Hindu conquest, where favored by social and physical circumstances, and which are now to be observed under the most various aspects, and often under highly interesting relations to the supervening people.

The general situation of the Khonds.

36. Exactly similar is the position of the neighbouring Sourahs, that of the Koles and that of the Cheutsoowars to the South of the Kistna, in the same range of Ghauts; that of the Goands which replace the Khonds on the West and North West, following the Vindhya chain across Berar; that of the Todawars of the pastoral tracts of the Neilgherry Hills, and the Currumbars at their bases, that of the Bheels of the Deccan and Central India, and innumerable others betwixt Nepaul and Comorin, which, with diverse institutions, manners, superstitions, tongues, and physical features, exist both unchanged, and at every stage of assimilation to the more civilized people.

37. The portion of the Khond race to which these observations refer is seen under the two situations which have been already attributed, in general terms, to the whole of this people South of the Mahanuddee.

38. It exists distinct, and virtually independent, in the region of mountain fastnesses, but at the same time intimately connected by alliance, and bound by various and powerful ties of interest and of feeling to the Zemindaries in which it is commonly said to be " included." Upon the other hand, it is seen in the tracts below the Ghauts, completely subjugated, and partially assimilated to the Hindu people.

39. In the former situation, it existed, completely cut off, by the interposed Zemindaries, from all relations with, from all knowledge of the successive Governments to which these were subject, until our assumption of Goomsur in 1836.

We first became acquainted with them in 1836.

40. No mythology nor legend appears to exist amongst the Khonds, which indicates, however dimly, their origin, or from whence they are derived, they believe themselves to have existed in Orissa " from the beginning," having either sprung from the soil itself, like the branch of the Greeks which traced it's origin to the Arcadian Pelasgus, or having been created contemporaneously along with it.

41. Their vague traditions, the scanty national annals of Orissa, the bare and uncertain records of the Zemindary families, and the surer evidence which is afforded by existing institutions, however, combine to establish, that the power of the Hindus was extended over the maritime and subalpine Territory originally possessed by the Khonds to the South of the Mahanuddee, partly by national, but principally by private enterprize ; and that advancing gradually, it reached the basis of the Ghauts about the 12th century whilst each leader of the encroaching race secured his conquests

Their expulsion by the Hindus.

* N B In Goomsur 5 Mootahs are entirely, two partially held on this tenure.

by the systematic assignment of lands* upon the tenure of Military service to the agricultural soldiery (the paiks of Orissa) by which they were achieved.

Their names.

42. The Hindu name for this people which we have adopted, " Khond" in the plural " Khondooloo," means mountaineer, from the Teloogoo word signifying a " hill." Their sole native appellation South of the Mahanuddee is " Koinga" or " Kwinga," which may be a corruption of " Kulinga," which, by the exchange of convertible letters may be Pulinda, meaning in Sanscrit and thence in Tamil " a barbarian," a savage mountaineer using an unintelligible dialect. They employ as distinctive *epithets* of their race, the terms—" Subboro" and " Mullaro," the latter signifying " hill people" from a root common to Tamul and Teloogoo, the Khonds designate the alpine portions of Orissa solely by its Hindu name (from that root) " Malwa," meaning " highlands." The Hindu people they call " Sassi," a word whose signification is not ascertained. The Khonds who inhabit the mountains are styled " Maliah Koinga," those of the low country " Sassi Koinga."

43. I proceed to state the exact relations which the portions of the Khond race are connected with, or included in Goomsur and Boad, bear to these Zemindaries.

SECTION II.

OF THE RELATIONS OF THE KHOND POPULATION OF GOOMSUR TO THAT ZEMINDARY.

Goomsur anciently divided amongst twelve Khandait Chiefs, who were subdued by the first Zemindar of the House of Bunje in the middle of the 9th Century. Khonds when expelled from the open country occupy wilder tracts of the Domain on servile conditions as " Bettiah" Khonds,—a portion of the Khond population of the basis of the Ghauts become free subject of the Zemindary or " Benniah" Khonds,—relation of the unsubdued mountain Tribes to the Zemindary.

The twelve Khandaits.

44. The annals of Goomsur, and those of Boad record, that, at the beginning of the 9th Century, the portion of the former Zemindary which is situated below the Ghauts, with the exception of a limited tract lying under the base of the mountains, was divided amongst twelve Chieftains, who bore the Orissan title of " Khandaits," the period and the circumstances of their establishment being unknown.

The first Zemindar of the Bunje family.

45. It is farther established, that about the year 1840, these petty Chiefs were successively reduced, and their Territories appropriated, by the first Rajah of Goomsur, the founder of the late line, who belonged to the Rajpoot family of Bunje, which had long ranked amongst the most powerful in Orissa : its branches then possessing the Domains of Boad, Mohurbunje, and Kunjeur, to which the Zemindary of Duspullah was ere long to be added.

46. The situation of the Khandaits plainly prescribed the complete dispossession of the primitive race of the Territory which they won from it. These rude and jealous Chieftains could have retained within their petty Estates, with no

views either of separate or of common advantage, any portion of a barbarous people organized by tribes and strongly animated by the spirit of independence. Whilst the location of their retainers throughout the country as an agricultural militia which afforded the security essential to the settlement of the industrious classes of a Hindu population, gave to their conquests immediate stability and value.

47. Accordingly in Goomsur below the Ghauts, the ancient race now exists only in scattered families which either occupy upon what may be termed servile tenures, tracts lost amid the forests, too wild, inaccessible, or insalubrious for the habitation of the Hindu, or dwell in petty hamlets whose services are assigned to particular villages or temples. **The Bettiah Khonds.**

48. I shall elsewhere describe minutely the situation of this class of the primitive people. Their condition is generally expressed by their designation "Bettiah" Khonds; this epithet meaning "labouring without hire."

49. The Khandait Chiefs, according to tradition, had acquired some degree of authority over the Khond population of the rugged and forest-laden skirts of the basis of the mountain chain, which however their divided power was unable completely to subdue. **The Benniah Khonds.**

50. The first Zemindars of the Bunje family, masters of an undivided authority, quickly reduced those tracts. But its inhabitants, perhaps from the advantages of their physical situation, perhaps from being peculiarly prepared to enter into such a relation by a long period of intercourse with their conquerors, secured a fortune entirely different from that which was the lot of the Khond population of the rest of the Domain. Instead of suffering expulsion or degradation, they were permitted to retain their lands either upon a rent tenure, or on condition of service to the Rajah, as free ryots, or as paiks, and their descendants now exist as free subjects of the Zemindary, becoming gradually assimilated to their conquerors they are designated "Benniah" Khonds, an appellation the meaning of which I have been unable to ascertain, although it is shared with a Hindu caste of Orissa.

51. Such appears to be the plain origin, and such are the distinctive features of the situations of the two classes of the Khond race which exist within the proper Domain of Goomsur. It remains to speak of the relations which exist between this Zemindary and the most important division of the ancient people, viz. the mountain Tribes.

52. The first Rajahs of Goomsur established, as the Chiefs of Boad appear to have done at a still earlier period, distinct and permanent relations (to which the rude, divided, Khandaits could not have been parties) with a considerable cluster of loosely confederated Khond Tribes which occupied the portion of the Ghauts bordering upon their Domain. A simple compact arose between them founded upon their only permanent common interests. It's sole object was, their mutual protection against the only class of enemies which was formidable to both, viz. the surrounding Zemindars; and it has endured, with the interest from which it sprung, essentially unchanged to the present time.

53. To understand distinctly the spirit of this simple contract, in connexion with what may be termed its external features; the forms which were either originally incidental to, or which have been since engrafted upon it, it is necessary to draw a clear line of distinction between the relative situations of the Khond Tribes and the Zemindary in a *political* and in a *moral and social* point of view.

54. The mountain Tribes had maintained their territories, and their liberties, against the utmost efforts of the Hindus. Their political independence was complete. They were as group of free societies, on a footing of perfect equality with the Zemindary, but they were, upon the other hand, morally in point of social advancement, in civilization far beneath it.

55. And the *principles* of the connexion which arose between them, and the outward forms which marked their intercourse necessarily sprang, respectively, from these two distinct and contrasted sources, namely, from their political relation which was marked by equality, upon the one hand, and from their relation in a moral and social point of view which was strongly characterized by disparity upon the other. And thus the external features of their relationship instead of reflecting its true character, are seen expressly to contradict it, making it easy for interest to misrepresent and almost inevitable for superficial observation to misconceive its real nature, and this alike in Boad and in Goomsur.

56. It is most important to understand distinctly the two following points upon which facts and forms are diametrically opposed.

57. 1st—The Military aids to the Zemindar which are given or withheld with perfect freedom by the Khonds bear much of the external character of "service," while they receive that designation exclusively from the Hindus.

58. 2d—The Tribes recognize the superior, social and personal rank of the Hindu Chiefs in contradistinction to their *authority* by forms which are nearly identical with those by which the latter acknowledge the political superiority of their paramount sovereign, and these forms nearly resemble those which attached in feudal usage to the incidents of "Homage" and "Investiture."

59. Hence the distinct and independent Khond Tribes of Goomsur and Boad have been regarded as forming an integral part of the population of each Zemindary, their territories are habitually styled "included"; they have been considered Vassals, not allies; and have been supposed to hold their free lands upon some species of tenure analogous to the feudal.

60. A late event established unequivocally the true nature of this relation. The Khond District, or rather half District of Hodzoghoro, lately transferred its attachment from Boad to Goomsur. This affair was the subject of frequent discussion while I was at Boad between the chief servants of the Boad Rajah, and the Khond Chiefs who visited me. The right of any Khond community to dissolve old and enter into new relations was not disputed on the part of the Zemindar. He

complained only of the loss, through the arts of Sam Bissye, of an old, subordinate ally whom he had never injured. The idea of the defection of a subject society, far less of the departure of a fief from its allegiance, was not for a moment contemplated. The Rajah had however put forward very different pretensions before I had an opportunity to institute exact enquiry.

61. In Goomsur, then it appears, that, under the operation of a few simple causes, the Khonds are divided into three principal classes; first, a servile class, the "Bettiah" Khonds; secondly, a class of free subjects, the "Benniah" Khonds, and thirdly, a class composed of independent Tribes which form a slightly confederated group, and are connected with the Zemindary by an alliance, the general nature of which (virtually the same as that between the corresponding parties in Boad) has just been indicated.

62. Besides these principal classes, the Khonds in the Eastern parts of Goomsur, and in the adjoining Districts, exhibit a number of minor subdivisions more nominal than real and founded upon slight differences in respect of manners, of mode of life, or of locality.*

* Vide Note.

63. In the next Section, after describing the relation which subsists betwixt Boad and its mountain Khond population, I shall notice exactly the incidents of Military Service, Homage, &c. (common to both Zemindaries) which are associated with it: and I shall then also endeavour distinctly to characterise the practical spirit of the connexion which subsists between the primitive people and the Hindu Chiefs.

SECTION III.

Relation of the Khond Population of Boad to that Zemindary.

Boad originally ruled by a Brahmin dynasty, which was replaced by the Bunje family. Its connexion with the Khonds made subservient to its general interests. Its relation to the Khond Tribes identical in its foundation, but different in practical spirit from that which exists between Goomsur and its hill Tribes, owing to the influence of two general causes. The mode in which Military aid is rendered by the Khonds to the Zemindars. The forms resembling those of Homage and Investiture. Maliah Khonds confer dress of Investiture on Zemindar.

64. The annals of Boad record, that it was ruled from a period of remote antiquity by a line of Brahmin Rajahs, the last of whom, in the ninth century, adopted as his successor a scion of the Bunje family, a brother of the Chief who conquered Goomsur from the Khandaits.

First Rajah of the Bunje Family.

65. It would appear, that no part of the primitive population has ever been permitted in Boad as in Goomsur, and in most of the neighbouring Zemindaries, to linger in its wilder tracts; whilst no portion of it ever became incorporated with the general population as free subjects, like the Benniah Khonds just described.

Connexion with Khond tribes made subservient to its general interest.

66. The Tribes, however of Kotrikia and Punchara, situated, respectively, upon the Eastern and the Western limits of the Domain, and the Tribe of Saat-mullick near its centre, have maintained their independence, at the sacrifice of their most valuable lands. In how far their preservation in integrity has been the result of accident, in how far of design, is unknown, but the fact has exerted a powerful influence upon the fortunes of the Zemindary.

67. The Domain of Boad, before the loss of its moiety to the North of the Mahanuddee above alluded to, extended for eight miles along the right, and for half that distance along the left bank of the river, where it breaks through the numerous ranges which here constitute the chain of Ghauts. In the great Valley which it thus included, ran the principal highway of commerce between a great portion of the Deccan and Central India, and the Coast of the Bay of Bengal; while there also flowed through it a constant stream of pilgrims from those regions to the Metropolitan shrine of Juggernaut; and, finally, this route became, in later times, the sole direct line of communication betwixt the capital of Berar and its Eastern Provinces.

68. It was necessarily a leading object of the policy of the petty Rajahs of Boad to strengthen, and to turn to the best account, the command of this important line of intercourse. And it was not difficult to render their connexion with the Khonds subservient to this purpose.

General and special relations to Khond Tribes.

69. A simple covenant of aid and protection indentical in its foundation, with that which has been described as existing betwixt the corresponding parties in Goomsur, appears to have connected, from a very early period the Chiefs of Boad with a slightly confederated group of Tribes which occupied the mountain region contiguous to the Domain.

70. The three Khond Districts above alluded to as situated on either side, or within the Domain, served to connect that group with the right bank of the river, and the formation of special engagements with the nearest Tribes, placed it in the power of the Zemindars to concentrate at any moment, upon any point of the Valley, large and scarcely tangible bands of mountain plunderers to act in concert with their own force of Paiks. The difficult pass of Burmool, the key of the Valley, could be held against any ordinary assault by a small party of these, aided by the Khonds of Kotrikia and those of the opposite bank of the river alone.

71. Thus the geopraphical position of Boad, so long as the Domain included both banks of the Mahanuddee, became in a great measure through the exclusive relations of its Chiefs with the Khonds, an unfailing source of consequence and of wealth. Productive tolls levied upon merchandize, pilgrims, travellers, and cattle, at the passes of the Valley, and upon the river, supplied a fund for the maintenance of a small mercenary force which rendered the Zemindar formidable to rival Chiefs, while complete exemption from State imposts was readily conceded by the Sovereigns of Berar, until the fall of the Mahratta Empire, as the price of secure communication betwixt their Eastern and their Western provinces—but whilst the original basis of the relationship between this Zemindary and the Mountain Districts

remained unchanged, the special compacts with individual Tribes which were necessary to secure their regular and cordial co-operation upon the line of the Mahanuddee, concurred with a general cause to which I shall next advert, to modify in an important degree the practical spirit of their connection, and to distinguish it from that which subsists betwixt Goomsur and its hill Tribes.

72. The change which took place in the relative strength of the Khond and the Hindu divisions of the population of Boad through the loss of Autmullick three generations ago, necessarily exercised an important influence upon the character of their connection.

Effect of change in the numerical proportion of the Khond and Hindu population by the loss of Autmullick.

73. Previously to that event, the number of the Hindus of the Domain was about half that of the ancient race; after it, the latter predominated as four to one. The rude Khonds felt with a new sense of power the ambition to exercise it, and, habitually united, under their federal heads, to interfere in the domestic policy of the Zemindary, which they were at particular junctures able to control certain Tribes adhered under every vicissitude to the Hindu Chiefs. The remainder appear now ranged against them in the bitterest hostility, now emulous in devotedness to their persons and interest; sometimes, upon the point of falling into vassalage, at others affecting a distant and independent interest, and in the prosecution of their objects combining indifferently with the domestic and the external enemies of the Zemindary. But the ever recurring necessity for mutual aid is seen to lead both parties back to the ancient footing of relationship, however widely they may have departed from it under the influence of temporary causes.

74. In Goomsur upon the other hand the Hindus have, until very recently, always borne to the Khonds nearly the same numerical proportion; that of about four or five to one; while the situation of this Zemindary has required the formation of no variable engagements with individual Tribes for special objects. We find in its simple history, the hill Tribes frequently summoned to render their aid to the Zemindar against hostile Hindu Chiefs; and, upon the other hand, they are often seen rallying around their federal Heads to defend their ancient rights against his encroachments. We see them, also, taking an active part in the internal discords of the Zemindary, and always appearing as forward partizans in the quarrels of the members of the ruling family. But, while their difficult position upon the plateau rendered them secure from conquest they were too weak to cope effectually with the power of the Hindu Chiefs; and thus the relative situation of the two parties remained to the period of our assumption of the Zemindary virtually unaltered.

75. Such is the general view which I have taken of the relations which at present exist between the Zemindaries of Goomsur and Boad and the Khond population which is included in each.

76. It remains only to describe under this head, the manner in which the Khond Tribes render Military aid to the Zemindars, and the forms by which they acknowledge their superior social rank.

77. When Military aid is required by the Rajahs of Goomsur, or of Boad, they communicate their desires, respectively, to the federal Patriarch of the cluster of Tribes connected with each; that Patriarch being, it is to be observed, at the same time the hereditary *agent* of the Zemindar for Khond affairs, and styled "Dora Bissye" in Goomsur, "Khonro" in Boad.

78. If there be no doubt as to the propriety of compliance with the demand, the Khond Patriarch at once sends his "arrow of summons" through the mountain vallies within his jurisdiction, and as it circulates like the Celtic fire cross, each house affords a fighting man—should the requisition, however, require consideration, the Patriarch summons a Council of Heads of Tribes, or of the whole people, as usage may prescribe, to determine the course to be pursued.

79. The federal Patriarch of Boad was always prepared to assemble a band of from 300 to 400 men, while he is said to have arrayed upon some occasions four thousand upon the side of the Zemindar.

80. The two forms by which the Khond Chiefs significantly recognize the high rank and social superiority of the Rajahs, are those to which I have alluded as resembling those which were associated with the feudal incidents of "Homage" and "Investiture."

81. The Patriarch of each Tribe attends annually, or once in two years, at the Hindu capital, to make a small offering of rural produce, and to perform his simple obeisance to the Rajah. This act of ceremony being repaid by equal courtesy, and by a gift of superior value.

82. Finally, the Heads of Tribes in Goomsur and in Boad, all accept, (although the usage is said to have originated at a period comparatively recent) "Saris," that is Orissan dresses of Honour and Investiture from the Zemindars. These they receive at any convenient period after their induction into their hereditary offices according to their own ancient forms; and they consider the ceremony to import simply the acknowledgment of their official position by the Rajah, from whom, however, they are pleased at all times to receive the slightest mark of honour; such as a dress, a gift, or a rarely bestowed title. In a word, they regard this form, as adding some degree of ornament but no manner of sanction to their ancient dignities.

83. It is lastly to be observed, in reference to this subject, that the Khond Tribes in each of these Zemindaries, send in their turn, to the Rajahs upon their accession, a similar silken Sari of investiture. The true signification of this form is of course differently interpreted according to the conflicting pretensions of the parties. But its acceptance is essential to the recognition of the Rajah by the Khonds.

84. With respect to the fulfilment by the Hindu Chiefs of the duty of protection towards the Khond Tribes, it suffices to say that they guard their nominally included territories, and their own proper Domains, with equal and jealous pride from every aggression by rival communities.

PART II.

Of the Usages of the Mountain Khonds relating to the Government of Society.

1. I have attempted to indicate the origin, and to state the conditions, and the spirit of the relationship which exists between the Zemindaries of Goomsur and Boad, and the portion of the Khond people which is included within their proper limits, or with which they are respectively connected. I shall now endeavour to describe the system of social existence, and of individual life, of the Mountain population.

2. According to my plan I shall speak, 1st, of the Usages of this Division of the primitive people; 2dly, of its Manners; 3dly, of its Religion. I shall afterwards attempt to enquire what measures ought to be adopted towards it.

3. It is, however essential carefully to premise, that whilst the principal conditions of social existence are the same in all the petty divisions of this remnant of the Khond race, those divisions are characterized by endless diversity in details. To describe their specific differences a separate portrait of each would be necessary. I propose to exhibit only what is general, and common to all, with what is practically important in individual and local usage.

4. It may, at the same time, be observed, that it is difficult to speak of the organization of these obscure Tribes, without employing terms which are indissolubly associated with the institutions of communities on a much larger scale, and at a stage of society much more advanced.

5. I propose to describe the Usages of this division of the Khonds, 1st, as they relate to the Government of society; 2dly, to public intercourse; and 3dly, as they appear in the place of Civil laws.

SECTION I.

Of the Divisions of Society and of the Patriarchal Authority amongst the Khonds.

The system of Khond society Patriarchal. Tribes and their sub-divisions with their Patriarchs. Federal Groups. Councils of Tribes and sub-divisions and of Groups. Of the Government of a Tribe. The basis of the Patriarchal authority. Partly founded upon birth, partly upon choice, partly upon religious feeling. The nature and the duties of the Patriarchal Office. Abbaya of a sub-division. Abbaya of a village. Descent of the Patriarchal Office. In case of non-age. Recognition of a Patriarch on his accession to Office.

6. The system of society which exists amongst the Khond population of the mountains of Goomsur and of Boad is in spirit and in form, as purely Patriarchal as that of any people to which accurate observation has extended. It is based, almost exclusively upon the principle of family. The spirit of equality pervades its whole The system of Khond Society Patriarchal.

constitution-society, is governed by the moral influence of its natural heads alone, to the entire exclusion of the principle of coercive authority.

Tribes and the subdivisions with their Patriarch.

7. This portion of the primitive people is composed, as has been already stated, of a number of distinct Tribes, which form loosely coherent Federal Groups slightly attached to each Zemindary.

8. Each Tribe possesses a distinct portion of Territory and is presided over by an Abbaya or Patriarch, who is the representative of its common ancestor. It is divided into several branches which are in like manner ruled by their family Heads; and finally these subdivisions are composed of a number of villages, each of which is governed by the lenial descendant of a chief chosen by it's first founders.

Federal Group.

9. Each cluster of Tribes is presided over by a federal Patriarch, who is the representative of a Chief the Head of a Tribe, who was anciently selected to represent and maintain the common interests.

Councils of Tribes and subdivisions.

10. The Patriarch of a Khond Tribe is aided, and controlled, in the management of its ordinary affairs by a Council composed of the Heads of its branches. These again have the Abbayas of villages for their assessors; while the village heads are assisted by the elders of their hamlets. Assemblies of the whole population of the Tribe, or of its sub-divisions, moreover, are convened, as usage may prescribe, under the directions of the Patriarchs of each grade, to deliberate upon general or upon local interests.

And Group.

11. The federal Patriarchs, in like manner, consult with the Heads of Tribes and assemble when necessary the entire population of the Federal Group.

12. Such is the theory of the social organization of this portion of the Khond people. But it is no where to be seen completely realized. Every conceivable deviation from the model occurs. As for example, two of the Districts of Goomsur (those of Bara Mootah and Athara Mootah) have now no Chief Patriarchs, their subdivisions being governed by their respective Abbayas without reference to common Heads.

13. The Khond people necessarily suffered very extensive and permanent disorganization during the contest with the Hindus, which ended in their gradual coercion, a broken remnant within the limits of the mountain chain. The Tribes, accordingly, are generally much intermingled, although some are said to remain distinct. But each now forms a social body of which the chief bond is the idea of natural affinity. While a common name, community of interests, of religious rites, of associations, and of traditions, render its sense of unity complete.

Of the Government of a Tribe.

14. I shall first describe the usages which regulate the Government of one of these rude societies, a Tribe ; and afterwards those according to which a confederate group is irregularly ruled.

The basis of the Patriarchal authority.

15. It appears that the patriarchal authority amongst the Khonds, although bearing but a single and uniform character, originally sprung from two distinct

services, viz. from the principle of family, which is the foundation of the office of Head of a Tribe and of its subsdivisions, and from the principle of selection, which is the origin of that of Head of a Village, and of a federal Group.

16. These two principles are now generally combined to form the basis of this authority, while its nature remains entirely unchanged.

17. The cause of this combination, and the mode in which it has been effected, are plain.

18. When, with the gradual growth and complication of public interests, and of private rights, the desire of order and secure enjoyment arises amongst rude Tribes ; the want of a public authority more powerful than that which the principle of family alone can supply is immediately felt ; and an attempt is made to remedy it generally in one of these two modes.

19. The first course is, to change the nature of the existing jurisdiction, to endow the Patriarch with prerogatives, enabling him to blend coercive with moral authority ; to convert the Tribe's father into a chief Magistrate. The second is, Part II.
maintaining the nature of the public trust unchanged, to provide security for it's more efficient exercise by the introduction of the principle of selection ;—by making personal fitness in addition to birth, a condition of it's tenure.

20. The Khonds have adopted the second of these alternatives. The Patriarchal Office, remaining hereditary as to family, has become virtually elective as to person, without having suffered any change in it's character. And herein consists a distinguishing peculiarty of the social situation of these Tribes. They have, I believe, attained the first objects of social union, the enjoyment of property, the fruit of fixed industry, in security and freedom, in a greater degree than any people which has been observed living under institutions which are in practice so strictly Patriarchal.

21. It is not difficult to perceive the degree, and the mode in which the principle of choice is here associated with that of family, to form the basis of the Patriarchal authority.

22. The supplementary principle of selection is generally combined with that of birth, in proportion to the importance of the trust for which it is desired to secure efficient depositories.

23. Thus the lineal Head is most frequently superseded in the case of the federal Patriarchs. For example, the late federal Head of Goomsur, Dora Bissye, was raised to that office on account of his superior abilities, in the room of his elder brother ; while in the case of Heads of Villages, whose duties nearly all are competent to perform, the regular course of succession is very rarely disturbed.

24. When a Tribe has determined that the chief authority shall devolve, not upon it's lineal Head, but upon another Member of the Patriarchal house more

competent to rule, nothing takes place, in any way resembling either a formal act of exclusion or of deposition. If the Patriarch has not yet assumed authority, he is passed over, as if by family arrangement. If he should have been recognized, he is gradually and silently superseded, retaining however much of his precedence.

25. And in neither case is a successor called to the management of affairs by any thing at all resembling election in the form which we associate with that term. The general will is manifested in the form of popular acceptance alone. The chosen Patriarch assumes the first place, and the chief authority, in virtue of the confidence and affection of the community which have rested upon him as the most worthy.

Partly founded upon religious feeling.

26. There is yet another source of the Patriarchal authority amongst the Khonds, viz. religious feeling.

27. The chief Civil and Sacerdotal Officers appear originally to have been united, or, at least, to have been always held by members of the chief Patriarchal family. At present, while the Patriarch, of whatever grade, is in same Districts uniformly, and in all occasionally the priest, the fortunes of his house are regarded as the chief Patriarchal index of the disposition of the Deity towards the society over which he presides, and hence he is the object of a certain degree of religious veneration, on the same principle upon which the Greek, the Teutonic and the Celtic Kings were venerated as the issue of Gods or of demigods.

28. It appears then, that the principle of family, the principle of election, and religious feeling combine, in proportions which vary endlessly, to form the foundation of the Patriarchal authority amongst the Khonds—I shall now advert to the *nature* of this authority, it's duties, and the spirit in which they are discharged.

The nature and the duties of the Patriarchal Office.

29. The Patriarch or Abbaya called by the Hendersamullicko of a Khond Tribe is simply the Head of a family of which every member is of equal rank, the first amongst equals—unlike the chieftain of a clan, he is in no respect raised above the community, whose interests, associations, traditions and manner of life he shares—none minister to his wants. He has no trace of state however rude; no separate residence or strong hold, no retainers, no property save his ancestral fields, by the cultivation of which he lives. He receives neither tribute nor aid, save perhaps an occasional harvest offering of good will. The enjoyment of the place of dignity at every public and private festival may be reckoned, as in the case of the Homeric Kings, amongst the most valuable, as it is amongst the most agreeable incidents of his situation.

30. The Patriarch of a Tribe, whatever may be the degree of his personal authority, undertakes no measures except in emergency, transacts no affairs without the assistance and sanction of the Abbayas, or of the assembled society. He has charge of the relations of his Tribe to the neighbouring Tribes and Zemindaries. He leads in war, and always accompanies the Military aids rendered to the Hindu Chiefs. At home he is the protector of public order, and the arbitor of private

wrongs;—conciliating feuds, and dispensing justice, but depending for obedience to his decisions, entirely upon his personal influence, and the authority of his assessors. He convenes council of the Abbayas, or of the whole Tribe, as usage may prescribe, either for deliberative, or for judicial purposes. He moreover discharges the local duties of Patriarch of his family subdivision, and Head of his Village.

31. The position of the Patriarch or Abbaya of a branch of a Tribe is, with reference to his more limited jurisdiction, exactly analogous to that of the Patriarch of a Tribe. Aided by the Heads of Villages whom he consults, and co-operating with the chief Patriarch, of whose councils he is a member, he contributes to the same general and local objects. He accompanies on all occasions the Military contingent of his Section.

Patriarch or Abbaya of a sub-division.

32. The Abbaya of a *Village* administers it's affairs in concert with it's elders. Thus aided, he endeavours to determine in the first instance all questions of slight importance relating to property or to order—upon him, in concert with the priest, devolves the important duty of providing for the religious ceremonies.

Patriarch or Abbaya of a Village.

33. Upon the failure of direct male heirs to the Patriarchal dignity in any grade, the Tribe, Branch or Village, elects from heirs general; and when the blood of the lineal Chief can be no longer traced, a *putative* brother is selected to inherit his lands and office, and the priest upon these occasions appears generally to direct the public choice, consulting, and declaring in oracular form, the will of the Deity.

Descent of the Patriarchal Office.

Part II.

34. In the case of temporary incapacity from non-age, or from any other cause, the next of kin on the male side, being a person of approved discretion, administers the Patriarchal office.

In case of non-age.

35. The sole form by which the Abbaya of a Tribe or of a branch, was anciently acknowledged upon his accession, consisted in presenting first to him, the liquor cup as it circled at a public assembly which met for his recognition, and for the completion of the funeral rites of the deceased Patriarch, upon the tenth day. His induction was completed by the priest, who by binding a yellow thread round his neck acquired a title to a trifling largess. To this ancient and simple acknowledgment of Patriarchal *precedence*, the Orissan form of official investiture,—the binding a silken band or "Sari" round the head of the heir, has been latterly superadded in most Districts.

Recognition of a Patriarch on his accession to office.

36. On the death of a *village* Patriarch all the Patriarchs of the branch meet with the population of the hamlet to recognize his successor, and by certain unimportant forms which vary in every District.

SECTION II.

The Public Assemblies of the Khond Tribes.

The public Councils of a Khond Tribe—arrangement—manner of discussion—Councils of sub-divisions and of Villages.

37. It thus appears, generally, that the ordinary affairs of a Khond society, whether relating to its public interests or to private justice, are conducted by Patriarchs of Tribes: of sub-divisions, or branches of Tribes, and of Villages, aided and controlled, the two former by the Abbayas of the next lower grade, the latter by the elders of each hamlet.

Assembly of a Tribe.

38. Assemblies of the whole Tribe, or of any of its sub-divisions, are convened, as was stated above, to determine questions of general importance. The members of every society, however, have a right to be present at *all* its councils, and to give their voices on the questions mooted; although the Patriarchs alone take a part in their public *discussion*.

39. I have received from several persons, both Khonds and Hindus, the following description of the mode of procedure at an assembly of a Tribe.

40. When occasion appears to the Heads of a Tribe to require a formal expression of the general will, the chief Patriarch sends a summons by the Panwas to every village to attend upon a particular day, at a central point, which is selected by him for the assembly.

Formation.

41. The nearer hamlets contribute their whole population to the council, the more distant depute the person or persons thought best qualified to represent them. The place of meeting is, generally, the open slope of a hill. The District Patriarch and the Abbayas of sections, first seat themselves in a circle. Around them, the Abbayas of villages form an outer ring. The rest of the community is arranged beyond, and all are armed—women and children sit apart, but within hearing distance.

Arrangement.

42. As the day advances, and the assembly begins to fill, the chief Patriarch rises from time to time to demand, whether such an Abbaya has taken his place? whether such an elder has appeared? or whether the men of such a village are prepared for their part? Despatches, messengers for some, chides others for delay, and receives replies, apologies, and explanations, loud and various in return.

43. The peculiar function of a Patriarch of the Tribe appears to cease with the completion of the assembly. He makes obeisance towards the four quarters of the globe, to the sun, and to the earth, and takes his seat in the circle of Abbayas of sub-divisions: He convenes the assembly, and is its most distinguished member, but he does not apparently regulate, or preside in any way over its proceedings.

Procedure.

44. In an assembly of a Tribe, the Patriarchs of the inner circle alone usually offer public counsel, and upon its formation, one of them immediately rises to

address the meeting. He begins, generally by touching upon some spirit stirring theme of the past,—the actions of a distinguished man, or the memory of a cherished event which bear some obvious relation to existing circumstances; and having by such preface prepared his auditory, he invites from amongst the crowd, within the inner circle, some elder of the people of venerable age and character, to bear testimony, as a living record, and as a depository of the traditions of the past, to the facts upon which the Chiefs shall found their respective councils.

45. The Abbaya then exhibits his view of the matter before the assembly, appealing, as he proceeds, to the reverend witness, who standing in the centre of the meeting, now avouches, now modifies his statements; or, taking the part of an interlocutor, maintains a dialogue with the speaker, or interposes episodes in his discourse,—while the assembly freely interrupts the Patriarch with loud tokens of applause or of dissent, but in all cases, it is said, without infringing the natural rules of decorum.

46. When the heads of the community succeeding each other in debate, have fully expressed their views, a plan of action in accordance with the general sense of the assembly is finally determined on, and declared by the Chief Abbaya; when the meeting is dissolved without farther formality.

Councils of Sub-divisions and of Villages.

47. No distinction exists amongst the Khonds, or appears to exist amongst any people at a similar stage of advancement,—between deliberative and judicial assemblies, in respect either of constitution or of forms of procedure. And when the Abbaya of a branch of a Tribe instead of consulting with the heads of Hamlets, formally assembles all under his authority, or whom the head of the village collects its inhabitants in familiar council beneath the appointed tree forms similar in spirit regulate the proceedings.

48. The jurisdictions of all these councils, however composed, are, of course entirely undefined. Those of each higher grade are simply supplementary to those below, deciding on matters which these have not sufficient weight to determine. Questions, however, relating to property in land, or to serious personal injuries, are referred to the Head of the Tribe and his Assessors. The rude forms of procedure which are employed in judicial enquiry are detailed in the Section which relates to the usages of the Khonds in the place of Civil Laws.

49. Such, then, is the mode in which a Khond *Tribe* is governed; by Patriarchs, patriarchal council, and popular assemblies; it being carefully remembered, that the social structure, and the whole body of usages which I attempt to describe, instead of being characterized by theoretical regularity and uniformity, are eminently local, fluctuating, and partial.

50. A Tribe is called a "Bengasikia" as the "Baska Bengasikia," or the "Jakso Bengasikia." "Baska" and "Jakso" being the names of the common progenitors. A branch of a tribe is distinguished by the name of its first Ancestor, thus *one* branch of the "Jakso" Tribe is called "Kooroo Jaksika," a village is

called "Nadzsoo;" a single family—"Roidoo" Khond names seem to be universally taken from natural objects, never expressing qualities. Thus there is the "Meeninga" or Fish Tribe, the Janinga or Crab Tribe, the Pochangia or Owl, the Syalinga or spotted Deer Tribe, the Orango or Nilgae. The land of a Tribe is termed its "Berunga."

I proceed to speak of the Tribes connected with Goomsur, and with Boad, in their Federal character.

SECTION III.

Of the Confederations of the Khond Tribes in Goomsur and Boad.

The basis of these unions. Each Group presided over by a Chief Patriarch, who is also the Agent of the Zemindar for Khond affairs. Duties of the Federal head of a Group as Agent of the Zemindar. The Dora Bissye of Goomsur. The Khonro of Boad. Federal Councils.

51. Dim and unsatisfactory traditions affirm, that the groups of Tribes which are included in Goomsur and in Boad, respectively, were united under the Ancestors of their present Federal Chiefs, previously to the establishment of any distinct relations between them and those Zemindaries.

The basis of these unions of Tribes.

52. However this may have been, their union is now, in each case, founded exclusively upon that connexion; the end of their confederation being the attainment of its first object, viz. protection from the Hindu Chiefs in return for aid, and the attainment, at the same time, of various secondary and accidental objects which have arisen out of it.

53. The constitution of these associations necessarily corresponds to this basis. Founded upon a single general and permanent interest which is weakly perceived, and upon several minor interests which are in the last degree partial, fluctuating and ill defined, these confederacies are, in point of structure, exceedingly imperfect and incoherent, while few institutions (which are exactly analogous to those of a Tribe) are feebly and incompletely developed.

Each Group presided over by a Chief Patriarch, who is also the agent of the Zemindar for Khond affairs.

54. Each Group of Tribes, as has been already stated, is presided over by a Chief Patriarch, the Abbaya of a *Tribe* whose predecessor was originally selected to represent and maintain the common interests. He is aided by Councils composed of Heads of Tribes, while for the decision of important questions, assemblies of the whole population are convened. I shall first describe the position and duties of a Federal Head, explaining the mode and the result of the combination of his office with that of Agent of the Zemindar in respect to his relations with the Khond Tribes. 2ndly. I shall advert to the peculiar objects of the Federal Councils.

Duties of the federal head of a Group.

55. The hereditary Head of a cluster of Khond Tribes exerts a powerful influence in society; the authority which he derives from birth being generally enhanced

both by the possession of superior abilities (the result of the principle of selection,) and by superior education. His first duty is the maintenance of the degree of union which is essential to the objects of the confederacy. He aids in the arbitration of all difficulties which do not yield to the authority of Patriarchs of Tribes. The settlement of boundary questions the most frequent sources of quarrel, are his especial care ; and he generally takes a part in the decision of all important disputes to which both Khonds and Hindus are parties. He is usually the sole channel of intercourse between the Tribes and the Zemindar in matters of importance ;—as with respect to Military aids, which he assembles, and, when on a considerable scale, accompanies to the field.

56. But the federal Chief, besides being the centre and bond of union of a group, generally heads it's partial leagues for special objects, when consistent with his own interest. When a few Tribes combine to vindicate a right, to revenge an injury or to gratify a passion, he lends his patriarchal authority to the movement, being seen, in fact, far more frequently directing the energies of a small part, than of the whole of the loosely aggregated confederacy over which he nominally presides.

As Agent of the Zemindar.

57. It was obviously the policy of the Hindu Chiefs to conciliate, and to attach by ties of interest and of feeling, these Heads of the unconquered remnants of the primitive race with which they formed relations ; and they appear, accordingly, at a very early period, to have induced them to accept the office of their agent for Khond affairs with which were enjoyed advantages and distinctions which the rude Patriarchs greatly prized.

The Dora Bissye of Goomsur.

58. Hence the federal Patriarch appears in each Zemindary, in the character of representative or hereditary agent, (designated in Boad by the Orissan term Khonro in Goomsur by it's synonyme Bissye) of the Zemindar, in respect of his relations with the Khond Tribes : and upon such conditions that he derives from this office a great increase of dignity and of influence.

The Khonro of Boad.

59. The Khonro, (who is the Abbaya of the Doobakkia Tribe) bears for the insignia of his rank, the Orissan symbols of a turban, a sword, a shield, a banner and a horse, and when Mahomedan styles penetrated the jungles of Orissa, the designation of " Omrah" was added with a grant of land, and in Goomsur, the head of the Jakso tribe represented by Dora Bissye, had a similar investiture. And the immediate descendants of the holders of these two offices all assume, respectively, the affix of " Khonro," or " Bissye."

60. The duty of these Patriarchs as the Agents of the Zemindars is this. It is their part to reside near them, to wait on them at their pleasure, to advise them on all that relates to Khond affairs, and upon every occasion to advocate their interests, and to vindicate their claims.

61. Now, so long as the duties and engagements of these two offices generally coincide, their combination, which makes it the interest of the chief Patriarch, for the enjoyment of his two fold dignity to reconcile the conflicting claims of the

Rajah and the Tribes, has generally a beneficial—a pacific tendency. But when their claims are irreconcileably opposed; when no compromise can be effected between them, or when the federal heads, as is frequently the case, are personally hostile to the Zemindars, this union of functions enables the former to act against the Hindu Chiefs, with the accumulated influence derived from both offices.

Tendency of this office.

62. The recent annals both of Goomsur and of Boad, present striking examples of such opposition arising from various causes, and of the expedients, which have been fruitlessly resorted to by the Zemindars with a view to remedy it.

Federal Councils.

63. For the consideration of questions which involve the common interests of each group of Tribes, public assemblies are held under the direction of the federal Chiefs exactly similar to the assemblies of Tribes.

64. Occasions for such councils have been afforded in Boad (in which Zemindary it may be observed that *all the conditions of federal existence* amongst the Khonds are most distinctly developed, and to which therefore *all the remarks under this head, bear more especial reference)*—by the disputed tenure of the office of Khonro; by the demand made by the Zemindar of a fixed aid from the Khonds when the Mahrattas first imposed tribute on him in the beginning of the century; and by frequent proposals at different periods for general pacifications.

SECTION IV.

Family of the Khonro of Boad and Dora Bissye of Goomsur.

The following notices of the families of the Khonro of Boad, and the Dora Bissye of Goomsur, are essential to understanding of their present position in each Zemindary.

Family of the Khonro of Boad.

Its traditions broken. Four brothers of the Doobakkia family came from the Zemindary of Kunjeur. The youngest brother head of the house. The third brother a Priest. The second brother a Naick. The elder brother a Messenger.

65. Sanguinary feuds in the chief house of the Doobakkia tribe have nearly broken the chain of its traditions. The following account of its origin, which is received by the best informed Khonds, is nearly as far as possible from being either satisfactory or consistent.

66. At an unknown period, but long previously to the establishment of the Bunje family at Boad, four brothers of the Doobakkia tribe emigrated thither at the express command of the Deity, from the districts of Chattaba Purbut, in Odnaat-ke-Naat, in the Zemindary of Kunjeur in Cuttack, and settled in the District of Atcombo.

67. The youngest, who was recognized as leader of the emigrant house, became federal Chief of the Khond Tribes of Boad, and was afterwards invested by the Zemindar with the office of Khonro. He is now represented by Nowbhun Khonro, the present federal Chief, from whose family, in the time of his father, the commission of Khonro was transferred by the Zemindar to the representative of the *eldest* branch of the house.

68. The third brother was a priest, and his descendant Narna Dehri, now ministers to the great Khond Divinity in the grove at Raneegunze.

69. The second brother received charge of the frontier post of Baringhi, the key of the mountain pass which connects Boad with Duspulla. He was designated "Naick" and is now represented by Suttiah Naick.

70. The office of the elder of the three brothers, suited, it is said, to his inferior capacity, was least in dignity, being that of messenger between the Rajah and the Khonro; whence the family designation of "Dundo," which is now borne by his descendant Madwa Khonro who, as above stated, holds the commission of Khonro of Boad.

71. The Naick possesses land at Baringhi. The Khonro, the priest, or Dehri and the Dundo, retain as an estate in common, the rich little valley of Raneegunze.

72. As much as it is essential to state of the genealogy of each of the branches of this house appears below.

Family of the Khonro of Boad.

4th House.—That of the Khonro—

Ooroodera.	Khonro.
Obero.	Khonro.
Gobera.	Khonro.
Godey.	Khonro.
Ramo.	Khonro.

Chultro.	Jugnath.	Khonro.	Molia.	Khonro.

Pudnaba.	Nowbhun K.	Gungodurra K. the

present representative who does not hold the commission of the Zemindar as Khonro, two sons.

3d House.—Of the Dehri—
Kartica Dehri,...... Donna Dehri.
Marna Dehri, the present representative.

2d House.—Of the Naick—
Paudava Naick, ... Goberdonno Naick.
Sattiah Naick, the present representative.

1st House.—Of the Dundo—
Poori Khonro.
Rutto Khonro, who first received commission of Khonro.
Bagwan Khonro.

Madwa Khonro, the present representative on whom the Zemindar has bestowed the office of Khonro.

FAMILY OF THE DORA BISSYE OF GOOMSUR.

It's primitive Seats—it's head resided at Koladah: compelled to retire to possessions under the Ghauts—assumed designation of Raj Benniahs. The distinction of Dora when acquired.

73. No distinct or consistent traditions cast light upon the early history of this family, which has from a period of unknown antiquity held a position in Goomsur, analogous to that of the Doobakkia family in Boad.

74. The primitive possessions of the Jakso tribe were situated in the Jaksowarri, Ootaragoda, Punchgoda and Berecote Mootahs, in the western division of Goomsur. Lying under the basis of the great mountain chain, they formed part of the tract whose population, as stated above,* was subdued by the early Bunje Zemindars, and acquired the designation of "Benniah" Khonds.

* Part I. para. 44.

75. The heads of the Jakso family resided where Koladah now stands. Rajah Bonomulli Bunje in the year* ..... slew its Partiarch "Kolah," and built the fortress which bears his name, when the Jakso tribe withdrew into Jaksowarri—many members of it having been destroyed in the year*...... by the first Rajah Dunoojee Bunje as sacrifices at the shrine of Kali, it was compelled to retire further south to Dodaramoonda, in the Mootah of Punchgoda, to Mojagoda, Berecote and Bybully; and these four places continued until recently to be their hereditary seats, while they held besides lands free, or at a trifling quit rent in the villages of Bhunjgherry, Puttaro, Gooripudro and Gullery.

* So in original.

76. Soon after the settlement of the Bunje family in Goomsur the Chief Khond house which closely affects Hindu manners, assumed the designation of "Raj Benniahs," which it has since borne. The distinction of "Dora" meaning "Chief" Bissye, was given by a late Zemindar of Goomsur to Kooli Bissye, uncle of Komolo Dora Bissye, the present head of the family, now a State prisoner. The latter received likewise from the same source the titles of "Runjeet" and of "Beerbob Patro" (by which last he was generally known) meaning "Chief of Angelic nature."

77. As much as it is necessary to know of the genealogy of the family of the Dora Bissye of Goomsur appears below.

Family of Dora Bissye of Goomsur.

Bassoo.	Bissye.
Ottye.	B.
Chumputto.	B.

- Sundoo B.
  - Orjunno B.
  - Mooliah B.
- Kooli B.
  - Samo B.
    - Kaptan B.
- Bulram B.
  - Gonisso B.
  - Onto B.
- Bonomulli B.
  - Purkito B. (killed.)
  - Komolo Dora B.
  - Sunko B.

(called the Buckshee) who is the present (a son by another mother) representative of the family and has two sons.

SECTION V.

Hereditary Hindu Officers of the Tribes of Boad.

Origin of this class of employes. Designations. In what Districts. Caste. Doogalos of Goomsur. Duties. Rank. The cas of the Mahalicko of Nowsagur. That of the Bissye of Hodzoghoro.*

* So in orig.

78. It remains still to notice under this head an institution, of comparatively recent origin, which exists amongst the Tribes which are at present, or were at no very remote period included in Boad.

Origin of hereditary Hindu Officers in Boad.

79. The relation betwixt these Tribes and this Zemindary having become (through causes which will be hereafter noticed) peculiarly complicated in the time of Rajah Beera Bunje, seven generations ago, a class of hereditary Hindu Officers was established to aid the Chief Patriarchs in the discharge of their duties,—particularly those relating to the external interests of their Tribes.

Appellations.

80. These employes received the Hindu appellations of "Bissye," "Mahalicko," "Naick," or "Dulbehra;" the two former of which are usually applied in Orissa to the civil managers of Districts, while the latter denote Military authority.

Where seen at present.

81. The four Districts of Chokapaud, Hodzoghoro, Bondoghor, and Bulscoopa, have at present Bissyes, and the latter had formerly, besides, a Naick and a Dulbehra. Descendants of former Bissyes of Oogdoor, Bagjeer, and Bara Mullick now exist in these Districts. In Nowsagur, of the Zemindary of Duspullah, there was until the other day a Mahalicko. In Dommo Singhi there is a Naick. In Tenteliaghor is a Dulbehra, by caste a Kheout or river fisherman, whose family has enjoyed great influence there from a very remote period.

Part II.

Object of their appointment.

82. The object of the institution of these offices was, to remedy the incapacity of the natural heads of Tribes for the conduct of such interests as required any considerable degree of knowledge of Hindu usages and manners by attaching by the ties of birth and of interest to each District, a person bearing a respectable

rank in Hindu society and sharing its civilization. And this class of functionaries was, accordingly, almost uniformly selected from the Soodoo caste, which is in Boad—the third in rank and which from its being almost exclusively engaged in the commerce of the hills was familiar with the language and the manners of the ancient people.

Endowed with Land.

83. These offices are hereditary in the direct line and are held during good behaviour. Valuable grants of land are attached to them, upon which villages formed of the families and dependents of the holders, uniformly spring up. The Bissyes, &c. are formally recognized as channels of intercourse by the Zemindars, who confer " Saris" upon them when they assume office, and generally court their friendship.

84. The first duty of an officer of this class, however designated, is the practical management, under the Abbaya, of the relations of the Tribe to Hindu society. It is his part to represent his Chief at the Petty Courts of the Zemindars, and to attend him thither, and elsewhere, upon all occasions when required, to interpret his language or to write for him. And finally, the ministry of the Deity adopted from the Hindu pantheon, and generally that of certain local Gods, is added to his cares.

Receive high considerations.

85. These functionaries uniformly enjoy a high degree of consideration amongst the Khonds. They have an honorable place in the public assemblies, at all private entertainments, and at religious festivals. When endowed with the talent which is requisite to sway the passions of their rude employers, their influence often predominates in their councils; and as arbiters in cases which the ordinary public authority is unable satisfactorily to determine, they often exert a very important power. But any semblance of pretension to independence, or forgetfulness of their subordinate situation in the Tribe, is promptly and indignantly resented.

Case of the Mahalicko of Nowsagur.

86. The Patriarch of Nowsagur in Duspullah thus spoke of the connexion of his Tribe with its Mahalicko, which had just come to an end. " He was," said the Khond Chief, " of an ill—disposed race, whom the Tribe had several times expelled, but was ever, to its misfortune, induced to receive back. He was first cast off many years ago, on account of his insolent pretensions to independence which were crowned by his stockading his village of Bonoe. His defences however were assaulted and burnt down, and himself driven with his adherents into Goomsur where he remained for twelve years. But in his absence," said the Patriarch, " the Tribe frequently felt the want of an arbiter in the last resort. The neighbouring Bissyes, and other Loodoos, interceded unceasingly in behalf of the banished Hindu, and pledged themselves for his future conduct, when his return was permitted. The Mahalicko however, forthwith re-established his stronghold and eventually implicated the Tribe in the crime of harbouring rebels from Goomsur. A Khond Tribe," added the Majee, " feels as a mother towards it's Loodoo dependents, and the family of Govind Mahalicko shall not want. But his office is abolished. We are more advanced than our forefathers were. I myself, I beg to represent have been educated, and frequently reside in the neighbouring capital of Duspullah, and we shall henceforth manage our affairs without Hindu aid."

87. The Bissyeship of Hodzoghoro was established under these circumstances.

88. Eight generations ago, the country which now bears that name, with the neighbouring tract of Tenteliaghor acknowledged, as it does at present, a common Khond Patriarch, and had for it's hereditary Hindu Counsellor the ancestor of the present Dulbehra of the latter District. Case of Sam Bissye of Hodzoghoro.

89. A son of the head family of the village of Bahmoonda, in the Mootah of Tarbutty of Boad, who were Soodoo hill traders, was, under circumstances variously narrated, entertained by the Khonds of this District at the suggestion of the Dulbehra, to minister to the God Peetabuldee. The new priest became a dealer in Mowhi flower and other spirituous liquors. His family by degree established a separate interest in the Western quarter of the District, and it's head was ultimately selected as "Bissye," by a division of the Tribe, and was recognized as such by the Zemindar of Boad.

90. It may be added, that the father of the present Bissye having quarrelled with the Boad Rajah, laboured to bring the Khonds of Hodzoghoro into connexion with Goomsur. And this object has been recently effected by his son Sam Bissye, who had further prevailed upon them to permit the late Rajah of the latter Zemindary to stockade his (the Bissye's) village of Pooranaghur, as one of the places of refuge, which apprehending the recurrence of collisions with the Government, he established amongst the then unpenetrated Ghauts. After the death of this Zemindar in rebellion, in the end of 1835, Sam Bissye of Hodzoghoro was the first after his rival the Dulbehra of the men of influence in the upper Khond country who tendered their submission; and he finally, through his influence with the Khonro, obtained the surrender of seveval of the rebel Officers of Goomsur who had found refuge in the Khond District of Ruttabarri in Boad.

91. This Hindu Bissye, the employe of a section of a Khond District, until now attached to Boad, has been appointed on our part, to take the place in Goomsur of the *federal Khond Patriarch,* the late Dora Bissye.

PART III.

Of the Usages of Intercourse of the Khond Tribes.

These Tribes have no idea of public rights or duties apart from express compacts. Ideas of duty towards our Government. Towards the Zemindaries in which they are included. Peace is their prevailing condition. Origin and cause of a Khond feud. That between portions of the Athara Mootah, and Burra Des in Goomsur. That between Beelscoopa and Dommosinghi. Khond contests intermitted.

1. The ideas which govern the mutual intercourse of the separate divisions of a people, and their intercourse with communities beyond their social sphere, must be understood before we can form a judgment respecting many important points in their character.

2. Amongst savage tribes the state of war is universal. At a mere advanced stage hostility is limited or modified by special compacts, but war is still the rule, peace the exception. At length the idea of pacific rights and obligations incidental to the mere fact of social existence, apart from ties either of natural affinity or arising from express covenants, is attained.

3. The Khond Tribes hold the views which belong to the second period of progress those which characterized the petty states of Ancient Greece, and until recently the clans of Scotland, which are now generally held by the Nomadi races of Central Asia, and which the most advanced Tribes of Southern Africa have scarcely attained.

4. Between Khond Tribes either as separate societies, or as members of a confederation when federal objects are not immediately concerned, the state and duties of peace are not presumed independently of convention either express or implied. And the Tribes alone which are associated in intimate alliance, restrain the conduct of their individual members towards each other, alone attempt to impose beyond their own pale, any restrictions upon man's natural privilege of acting for himself. The idea of social rights or duties has never entered into the conceptions of these Tribes with respect to communities to which they are attached by no natural or artificial tie, which are beyond their system, as are the Zemindaries with which they have no direct relations, or as was our power when it's existence was first made known to them. And it is obvious that in any case to punish them for the non-existence of those ideas, were to punish them for a necessary state of their minds.

5. With the Zemindaries in which they are included, they are according to these views bound to peace alike in their federal and in their individual character. So long as the terms of alliance are observed by the Hindu Chiefs, but upon their infraction, the right of war returns.

6. Hence while within each Tribe order and security prevail, beyond, all is discord and confusion ; every where is seen an incipient, or a dying feud, and every Tribe has an unsettled account with the Zemindar.

7. But at the same time the general circumstances of the situation of most of these Tribes, and the ideas and feelings upon which their manners are mainly founded determine them powerfully to pacific habits ; producing frequent alliances and tending every where to soften hostility.

8. In a word the practical spirit of their intercourse, is the result of a conflict between the anti-social spirit of independence which universally characterizes rude people, and the love of security and enjoyment which necessarily attends the hereditary possession of competence and freedom, while, upon the whole, the latter influence predominates.

9. It is indeed manifest, that in a country composed of chains of open unprotected vallies thickly peopled, and teeming with every form of rural wealth, peace although broken and uncertain must be the prevailing condition.

10. The feuds of races divided into *clans* generally spring from the passions or the caprices of the Chiefs. Under Patriarchal institutions as they here exist, where the great characteristic of society is equality where the acquisition of Territory is little desired by heads of Tribes without retainers, and where the Military spirit is subordinate to the spirit of industry enmities generally arise out of questions of individual right.

11. The common origin and course of a Khond feud are as follows.

12. A field or a farrow's breadth of land is disputed upon the border of a District and gives rise to rustic strife between the parties and their respective hamlets, when blood is split, and retaliation by relatives ensues should the Tribes to which the disputants belong be disposed to hostility they speedily embrace the quarrel, but should friendship be the prevailing sentiment the Patriarchs on both sides, aided perhaps, by the federal Chiefs, meet to compose the strife: and in this case, even should it have been already espoused by the two *sub-divisions* within whose limits it occurred and have produced feelings of animosity in them too strong to be immediately allayed, the dispute generally remains confined to these limits.

13. Thus a conflict has been maintained time out of mind, in the Goomsur Maliahs between the sub-divisions of Courminghia and Potlinghia of the District of Bara Mootah and those of Persikia, Gersingia and Dokeringia of that of Beerree Des, without involving in any considerable degree the remaining portions of either.

14. The following is the history given by both parties of the contest which at present divides Beelscoopa and Dommosinghi.

15. A Hindu of the Mhanti caste who had long resided in Dommosinghi claimed a piece of land adjoining his own which was held by the Khonds of Beelscoopa—to be within their frontier, supported by his village, he carried his plough into the disputed field, but after a conflict of clubs was compelled to retire. The Mhanti reinforced by a strong and well armed band from the neighbouring hamlets, returned next day to make good his pretensions, but was again repulsed after a contest in which one man was killed and many were wounded. After a long period of strife during which a considerable part of either border was wasted, the Hindu supported by the leading Khonds of the sub-division proceeded to Beelscoopa and besought the support of the Bissye.

16. That officer obtained the convention of a general council, urged the claims of the Mhanti as a dependent foreigner to protection, reminding the assembly of its many ancient causes of feud with Dommosinghi, and of the decided inferiority of that District in point of strength. It was unanimously determined to espouse the cause of the Hindu—Beelscoopa assembled its fighting men, and within three days every village of Dommosinghi was fired and thirteen of its inhabitants slain. The progress of this feud was arrested with nearly all the engagements of society in these Districts, by the appearance of our troops above the Ghauts.

17. The feuds of Khond Tribes while they rarely die, seldom proceeds to extremities, never I believe to the destruction of a Tribe and the seizure

of its lands, and they are, in general, entirely intermitted (as is the case amongst the Affghans) when either party from any cause whatsoever, ceases, even temporarily, to assert the disputed right. Thus, the sanguinary conflicts of the Districts of Bondoghor and Sarunghur in Boad, for the possession of certain border
Part 3. lands, slumber during the hot weather and the rains, awaking to fresh rage at seed time and harvest. And the boundary feuds between the divisions of Hodzoghoro which are under the influence of Sam Bissye and the Dulbehra respectively, give rise only to an annual fray upon the trying occasion of a solemn offering of human sacrifice made at the same time by both parties to the God of Limits upon the disputed frontier.

PART IV.

Of the Usages of the Khonds in the place of Civil Laws.

1. From what has been stated in the preceding part of this paper it is plainly to be inferred that between members of different Khond Tribes, retaliation is in general, necessarily, the sole remedy for wrongs of whatever order. But each society interposes to prevent the exercise of the natural right of revenge within it's pale, by a rude system of compensatory justice, which has in view exclusively, the private satisfaction of individuals not the vindication of any moral or civil rules of right. The main provisions of this system are the following.

Of Offences against the person.

Murder, Homicide, Manslaughter and Wounding.

2. In cases of murder, the Khonds recognize the right of blood, revenge in the kindred of the deceased, and like the Bedouins, regard the exercise of this right as a duty; while unlike them, they consider the acceptance of compensation as in no case disgraceful.

3. The right to revenge blood appears to extend to relatives within a degree of affinity not strictly determined; and it's existence certainly renders murder a rarer crime among the Khonds, (as amongst the Arab Tribes) than the state of manners would lead us to anticipate.

4. When the revenge of blood is foregone, the entire personal property of the murderer is awarded, in compensation to the representatives of the deceased, and it was uniformly asserted by my informants, that similar compensation is made in all cases, both of excusable homicide and of manslaughter.

5. In cases of wounding equivalent in property is adjudged if the injury be severe, or of a lasting nature, but not otherwise.

6. In every case however, the injured party has a right to subsist in luxury and the expense of the offender, during the period of convalescence. For wounds,

however serious, given under circumstances of extreme provocation, or in a drunken squabble, slight compensation is awarded.

2.—Of Offences against Property.

Theft. Wrongful occupations of the Soil.

7. In cases of theft or of robbery, the restitution of the property abstracted or the substitution of an equivalent is alone required by Khond usage upon the first offence. But expulsion from the society follows upon it's repetition—this crime is not very common among the Khonds, save in a few particular tracts, that for example of Gonzabadzoo in Goomsur.

8. When stolen agricultural produce cannot be recovered, the injured party is put in possession of the land of the plunderer, until it's produce replaces his loss; one half of the crop being placed annually to the credit of the offender.

9. Unjust occupation of the soil, for whatever period is remedied amongst the Khonds, by its simple restoration, without compensation.

3.—Of Adultery.

Adultery where established by the testimony of the husband.

10. A husband in case of adultery established by his ocular testimony, has a right to put the adulterer to death; and for this offence there is no composition. The adulterous wife (not regarded as the property of the husband) is punishable only by dismissal to her paternal home, and this may be inflicted upon sufficient proof of her guilt by any species of testimony.

4.—Law of Inheritance.

Of landed property and agricultural stock. Moveables. In case of failure of heirs.

11. Landed property and agricultural stock descend exclusively in the male line, females being incapable of holding land.

12. In most Districts the eldest son receives an additional share of both of these species of property; in a few they are equally divided. In case of failure of issue, brothers inherit equally, and then the brothers of the father as the Salique law.

13. Daughters divide equally personal ornaments, household furniture, money and moveables, while their brothers are obliged to maintain them, and to contribute equally to the expense of their marriages.

14. On the failure of heirs male, land becomes the property of the village, and is divided among its members.

5.—Law of Property in Land.

Land possessed without Tenure. Waste Land.

15. Land is possessed by the Khonds without tenure, the right of possession being simply founded in the case of Tribes upon priority of appropriation and the case of individuals upon priority of culture.

16. The usages of different Districts in respect to waste land vary much.

17. In some quarters I found the waste land partition amongst the villages but in others not. The exclusive use of unreclaimed land for pasturage or for jungle produce, was, however, in no case asserted, and, generally, few practical restrictions existed as to the occupation of waste by individuals within the boundaries of his Tribe.

6.—Rules relative to the transference of Land by Sale.

18. The forms observed in the transfer of land by sale are these.

19. The selling party intimates his purpose to the Abbaya of the Section, not to obtain his sanction, but to give publicity to his intentions. He then goes with the intending purchaser to the village in which the property is situated, and summons five respectable inhabitants to bear witness to act of sale.

20. When assembled on the land to be transferred, the seller calls upon those witnesses, and at the same time solemnly invokes the Village Deity, to bear testimony, that a portion of land specified is alienated by him, for ever, to a certain person, for a certain consideration. He then delivers a handful of soil to the purchaser who in return makes over part of the purchase money when the transaction is complete. The close similarity between the forms, which obtain among this people, and those which are employed by the nations of Europe and of Western Asia, to give publicity and certainty to transfers of real property, is sufficiently striking.

7.—Procedure of Judicial Councils.

Procedure in deciding questions of property in Land, and the greater offences against the person. Inquiry by testimony on oath, and by ordeal. Costs of suit.

21. Questions of property in land, and of the greater offences against the person, are generally decided with much solemnity, by councils of elders convened by Head of Sections or of Districts, and by the examination of witnesses, and of the parties, to both of whom an infinite variety of oaths are administered while they are occasionally subjected to ordeals.

22. Of judicial tests the two most sacred are founded on the belief that rice moistened by the blood of a sheep killed in the name of the Earth God will, if

eaten by litigants, destroy the perjured, and that a portion of disputed soil made into clay will, if swallowed by them, have a similar effect.

23. The former test in which the great Khond Deity is adjured, is resorted to only upon the most solemn occasions. The common oaths of the Khonds are upon the skin of a Tiger, from which animal destruction to the perjured is invoked upon a Lizard skin, whose scaliness they pray, may be their lot if forsworn; upon the earth of an ant hill, like which they desire that, if false, they may be reduced to powder, and upon a peacock's feather while the universal ordeals of boiling water, oil and hot iron are constantly resorted to. Boundary lines when determined by public tribunals are marked by stones set up with renewed sanctions, in presence of the Abbays.

24. The liberal entertainment of the members of every tribunal with rice, flesh and liquor, at the conclusion of its proceedings, falls in all cases as costs of suit, upon the losing party, an arrangement it may be observed, the reverse of that which obtains amongst the Bedouins.

PART V.

Of the Manners of the Mountain Khonds.

I have attempted to describe the relations which these rude Mountain Tribes bear to Hindu society, their social organization, their rules of public intercourse, and their civil usages. I proceed to speak of their " Manners," including under this head the more prominent features of their moral and intellectual character, and the general habits which result therefrom.

SECTION I.

Of the Paternal authority among the Khonds—their Industry.

The strength of the paternal authority. System of family life. Sons cannot possess property before their father's death. Practice agriculture alone. Hindu castes settled on the hills. Manner of labour. Rich in agricultural stock. Hill produce. Market value of land—mode of exchange.

1. In contemplating the manners of the Khonds, attention is first arrested by the extraordinary degree of purity and strength in which the principle which governs society—that of paternal authority, is seen at its source,—in the bosom of each family.

2. There it reigns nearly absolute. It is a Khond maxim that a man's father is his God, disobedience to whom is the greatest crime—and all the members of a family live united in strict subordination to its head until his death. Before that event a son cannot possess property of any kind. The fruits of his labour, all his acquisitions go to increase the common stock, and the form and sense of family

unity are further preserved by the remarkable usage, according to which all the sons of a house (with their wives and children) continue, while their father lives, to share the Patriarchal board, prepared by their common mother. The married sons, however, necessarily occupy separate houses, with the exception of the youngest, who never quits his father's roof.

3. The outward order of Khond society; all it's conditions, its texture, and its colouring necessarily derive their distinctive character chiefly from the ideas which produce, or which spring from this remarkable system of family life.

Practice agriculture alone.

4. The Khond population in these Districts is distributed in the proportion of about sixteen inhabitants to a square mile, over a country which is entirely partitioned amongst the different Tribes, but of which not an eighth part is appropriated by individuals, while a large portion of the remainder is capable of yielding rich returns to laborious industry, and is open under few limitations to the first occupant.

5. The law of inheritance, upon which the distribution of property mainly depends, is eminently favorable to individual industry. Every Khond son, as above stated, receives an equal share of the property in the soil and in agricultural stock which has been accumulated during the life time of his father.

6. And whilst nature and this most important law thus favour industry it appears that the Khonds, in place of any trace of the characteristic sentiment of barbarism—that labour is at once an evil and a degradation, have from time immemorial regarded the occupation of agriculture, varied by the pursuits of war and the chase, as almost exclusively honorable. The only exception being in the Southern Districts, and in favour of the arts of working in iron and in clay.

7. Hence, there exists amongst this people, generally speaking, but a single class, that of allodial proprietors of the soil; there being no renters of land, nor labourers for hire, and it may be observed, each petty freehold consists of a portion of the irrigated soil of the valley which is minutely sub-divided, and of a tract of the upland which is held in much larger portions.

8. The practice of the art of agriculture exclusively, by the mountain Khonds, with the partial exception above noticed, is rendered possible by the settlement in these Districts of families of the following Pariah or Hindu castes, who manufacture first necessaries, and perform other indispensable services.

Pariah and Hindu castes settled on the Hills.

1. The Panwa or Weaver.
2. The Lohara or Ironsmith.
3. The Komaroo or Potter.
4. The Gouro or Herdsman.
5. The Soondi or Distiller (in the Eastern Districts.)

9. Of these, the Panwa is proverbially indispensable to every Khond hamlet. His duties are to provide human victims, an occupation which is however restricted

to certain families in which it is hereditary; to carry messages, such as summonses to council or to the field; to act as musician at ceremonies, and to supply the village with cloth, of which the Khond allowance is a yearly garment.

10. These castes, which have been settled in the Khond country from time immemorial, all partake of food which has been prepared by the Khonds, who will not however eat from their hands. They use both the Khond and the Ooriah languages. They appear to have their own Gods to whom they sacrifice and they are not allowed to participate in the worship of the Khonds. By these, they are treated, particularly the Panwas, with great kindness, but as an inferior, and protected perhaps as a servile race. They are never neglected at a feast: and any injury done to them is promptly resented. But they are never allowed to bear themselves as equals. And they can in no case hold land. They generally maintain their blood pure.

Manner of labour.

11. Agriculture is practised by the Khonds with a degree of skill and energy, which is perhaps no where surpassed in India, and which has produced a degree of rural affluence rarely paralelled.

12. At the season of labour, the Khond rises at day break. Before quitting his cottage, he eats a full meal, consisting of Moong Raggi or Tuar, boiled with a portion of junge herbs, and flavored with a piece of goat's or swine's flesh. Then yoking his team or shouldering his axe, he goes out for the day. When employed in ordinary work, as at the plough, he labours without intermission until three o'clock in the afternoon, when he bathes in the nearest stream. But when his toil is more severe, as in felling wood, he rests to eat a mid-day mess which is brought to him to the field. At evening he returns home to a meal similar to that of the morning with the addition of liquor of tobacco. At harvest and seed time, the women share in every form of field labour and where there is no Hindu cowherd those of each family watch the village cattle by turns.

Rich in agricultural stock.

13. The Maliah Khonds are extremely rich in every species of agricultural stock. They have large herds of bullocks of a small breed, and of buffaloes, numerous flocks of fine goats and abundance of swine, and every hamlet teems with poultry.

Hill produce.

14. Rice of several sorts, of various oils, millets, pulses, and fruits, with tobacco, turmeric, and mustard of superior quality, are the most important species of hill produce, and these the Khonds exchange with resident merchants, principally of the Soodoo caste, or at the fairs of Koladah and Corundah, aided in their bargain making by these Panwas, and for salt, cloth, brass vessels and ornaments, and a few other necessaries.

Market value of land.

15. Transfers of land by sale constantly take place in these Districts, and the value of a piece of ground at Borogootza, which required four bullocks for its cultivation and sufficed for the support of a family of four persons, was estimated by some intelligent Khonds at from 40 to 50 pairs of bullocks, while I was told by an inhabitant of Borapall in Nowsagur, that it would fetch at least as much if situat-

ed in that District. This being with reference to the rent of land in Boad, as nearly as could be judged, about 10 or 12 years purchase, and a village of Beelscoopa which was sold by its Abbaya, and inhabitants, as having become unlucky, to a rich Khond from Chokapaud, brought a price which was in keeping with this estimate.

Medium of exchange.

16. The use of money, with the exception of cowries, was until recently, nearly unknown to the Maliah Khonds, and the value of all property is estimated by them in "lives," a measure which requires some adjustment every time that it is applied, a bullock, a buffaloe, a goat, pig or fowl, a bag of grain, or a set of brass pots being each with any thing else that may be agreed upon a "life." A hundred lives, on an average, may be taken to consist of ten bullocks, ten buffaloes, ten sacks of corn, ten sets of brass pots, twenty sheep, ten pigs and thirty fowls.

SECTION II.

Other elements in the character of the Khonds.

Universal hospitality. Meriahs not guests. Involuntary Guests. A Tribe may become guests. Love of personal independence. Attachment to persons not to institutions. Fidelity and public engagements. Endurance of physical suffering. In some Districts Chiefs read and write. Nawbhun Khonro. Dora Bissye.

Universal hospitality.

17. It is a highly striking and important feature in the manners of the Khonds that the ideas and sentiments which give rise to the usage of universal hospitality exist among them in the highest vigor, producing effects exactly analogous to those which are seen amongst the people of Western Asia.

18. Hospitality is regarded as one of the first duties. It is equally imperative upon all. "For the safety of a guest," say the Khonds, "life and honor are pledged, he is to be considered before a child." Every stranger is an invited guest, and any person may acquire, under any circumstances the privileges of the character by claiming them. No person, whether Khond or Hindu, can appear at a Khond Village without being invited to enter, and the burden of public hospitality does not fall more upon the Abbaya than upon any one else. There is no limit to the period to which hospitality may be claimed, a guest can never be turned away, and his treatment must be that of a member of the family. Fugitives upon any account whatever from other Tribes, must be received and protected. Meriahs however cannot claim refuge as guests. They are given up as property amongst friendly Tribes. In unfriendly ones they generally find an asylum, a person who has sought refuge is supported until he can make up his mind to return to his Tribe, or to seek adoption into that of his host, and in the latter case he generally labours on the land of his protector until he can procure a share for himself.

Meriahs not guests.

Involuntary guests.

19. If a man can make his way by any means into the house of his enemy it is considered a case of refuge, and he cannot be touched, even although his life has been forfeited to his involuntary host by the law of blood-revenge. I heard of a

Panwa, who having killed the son of the Abbaya of his village, fled and escaped vengeance. Two years after he returned, and in the middle of the night rushed into the house of the Abbaya. A Council of the Tribe, any one of whom would have previously destroyed the murderer, determined that he must be regarded as a guest, and he was accordingly permitted to remain unharmed. Sometimes, however, when an enemy thus makes himself a guest the house may be vacated and food may be refused to him and he may be killed if he comes out. But this proceeding is very rarely considered justifiable.

20. One Tribe must receive another if it become fugitive. Two branches of a Tribe having fallen out at a feast, fought until one was driven from its lands, of which with the villagers, the other part took possession. The expelled branch sought refuge with another Tribe, and was supported by it for a year. In the end, an Abbaya of the victorious portion relented, and secretly became a party to a scheme for the readmission of the others. He sent them notice, when the watch which was kept for their exclusion was somewhat relaxed. The people rushed into one of their old villages, from which as guests it became impossible to expel them, and they at last obtained possession of their lands.

A Tribe may become guests.

21. The family of the Rajah of Goomsur were considered by the Khonds to whose care he confided them, in the light of guests, in the most sacred sense, and this was in a great measure the origin of our first quarrel with these people.

22. This spirit of personal independence, and the spirit of attachment to persons rather than to institutions, are very powerfully developed in the character of these rude people.

23. In the former trait, is seen the wild and passionate love of individual liberty which distinguishes the barbarian, but partially subdued by the civilizing influences which universally attend upon the hereditary possession of competence with freedom.

Love of personal independence.

24. But the ideas of the Khond are necessarily few, vague and perplexed. His convictions are, save on a few points, weak, uncertain and confused, and with his childlike reason is combined maturity in passion.

25. Hence, he is not unfrequently seen to gratify his appetites, to indulge his resentments, or his revenge with the selfishness, the brutality and the head-strong fury of the barbarian.

26. The Khond is attached not to his tribe, Branch or Hamlet, but to his Abbaya, his family head and the tie by which he is bound to him, may compare as above observed for strength, and for simple beauty, with any that is to be found in the relations of mankind.

Attachment to persons not to institutions.

27. The genuine instinctive spirit of savage freedom still occasionally shews itself in these people as in the preference of death to the endurance of the least restraint. A Khond, captured by our Troops in Baramootah, immediately tore out his

tongue by the roots and died, another made prisoner after maintaining a long and gallant conflict with a horseman, until he was stabbed by another assailant from behind, sternly refused food and perished on the fourth day.

Fidelity and public engagements.

28. The annals of Boad attest that fidelity to its public engagements is an eminent virtue of this race. The history of the connection of Kotrikia, Beelscoopa and other Districts with that Zemindary, breathes the spirit of honorable obligation, characteristic of the compacts of feudal society.

Endurance of physical suffering.

29. Our contest with the Khonds in Goomsur arose out of their faithful redemption of a solemn pledge to its late Zemindar to give hospitality to his family and to save its honour.

30. Its melancholy course established, that in superiority to physical suffering, the Khonds are surpassed by no people of whose manners that virtue has been the boast. In a period of suffering rarely paralelled, during which the population of Baramootah wasted for two months beneath famine, disease, and the sword, no single Khond was found to falter in his devotion to the common cause, and when at length the fathers of that tribe were betrayed and condemned to die with what admirable courage, what affecting resignation, what simple dignity, did they meet an ignominious fate, on the sites of their ruined homesteads.

31. The Khond Patriarchs are very proud of their race. Even when they most affect Hindu customs, they delight to assert their superiority to the more civilized people. Their most common boasts are, that they reverence their fathers and mothers whom the Hindus treat with contempt. That they are men of one word whilst Hindus are false and uncertain. That the Khonds are one as a race, while the Hindus are endlessly subdivided. They have the easy bearing of men who are unconscious of inferiority and rarely employ expressions of courtesy. In salutation they raise the hand perpendicularly above the head—in meeting on the road the younger persons says " I am on my way," the elder replies " go on."

32. The Khond appears to possess a clear and vigorous intellect. He is slow of deliberation, but prompt to act. His character is marked by the most determined spirit of perseverance, and is in a great measure free from the puerility, which is the great blemish of that of the Hindu.

33. In the Districts with which I am best acquainted, which however, are those which most intercourse with the low country, the Chiefs readily embrace any opportunity to acquire all that is learnt by the Hindus.

In some Districts Chiefs read and write.

34. In the small valley of Borogootza, for example, three Abbayas read the Shasters with considerable ease. An intelligent Sunnyasi who resides there instructs a good many Khond children with his own in letters, and ascribes to them a capacity quite equal to that of Hindu children of any caste. The Manjee of Nowsagur in Duspullah has learnt all that is generally taught in that Zemindary: and the Patriarch of Punchora who entertains a number of Soodoo priests at his chief village is said to be well-informed in the doctrines, and strictly observant of the

ceremonies of the Hindu religion. I first met Madwa Khonro at Raneegunge, seated at his door engaged in teaching his child to read.

35. Nawbhun Khonro, chief Patriarch in Boad, was educated with the sons of the Zemindar. The intelligence, courage, and determination which he has displayed in vindicating, during a long life what he deems to be his rights, against that Chief, have obtained for him the respect of every Khond. **Nawbhun Khonro.**

36. Dora Bissye, chief Patriarch in Goomsur, commands to a great extent the admiration both of the Hindu and the Khond population of the Districts which lie between Kimidy and the Mahanuddee, and he is well known beyond that river. He is the object of feelings of the deepest veneration to his own race in Goomsur, Duspullah and a great part of Boad. And having had opportunities of observation, I may state, that my estimate of his character justifies the opinion of those before whom his life has been spent. **Dora Bissye.**

37. This remarkable man, it may not be out of place to observe, is in his 57th year, and although careworn, is still vigorous. In person he is somewhat below the middle size, according to the Hindu standard; of spare habit, and, by no means robustly formed. His physiognomy is spirited, and when excited intellectual, but with a predominating expression of benevolence. His features are regular, sufficiently bold for expression, but by no means striking, and not strongly marked by the peculiarities of his race. His manner is animated, perfectly self-possessed, and very pleasing. He might pass for a well-bred Brahmin of Orissa.

38. His views upon every subject on which he is informed are clear and discriminating; and he perceives new facts and their relations, with remarkable facility. His habits not being Military (as is also the case with Nawbhun Khonro, chief Patriarch of Boad) cowardice was vulgarly imputed to him in our camp as if a people ever lavished its affections upon a poltroon.

39. Having passed his time by turns amongst the Khond vallies of the Ghauts, and the petty Courts of the Zemindars, he is as well informed of all that relates to the Hindu population of a considerable portion of Orissa as of the usages and interests of his own people. He is well read in the Puranas, and forgot his prison in enquiring of the present state of the jewelled place of Lunka. His personal habits are those of an Orissan Brahmin, and he is attended exclusively by persons of this caste.

SECTION III.

Of the Relations of the Sexes and Domestic Ceremonies.

Influence of women. Regarded with respect. Who can marry. The wife older than the husband. The wife not the property of the husband. Polygamy and concubinage. Observance of marriage tie. Drunkenness disgraceful. Births. Deaths.

40. Women, among the Khonds, appear to enjoy a degree of social influence, at least equal to that which has been attributed to them in the Patriarchal communities of Western Asia. **Influence of women.**

Regarded with respect.

41. They are almost uniformly treated with respect,—the mothers of families generally with much honour. Nothing is done either in public or in private affairs without consulting them, and they generally exert upon the counsels of their Tribes, a powerful influence favorable to humanity.

42. " Our women are not deficient in intelligence," said the fierce old Bagwan Sow of Baramullick, " but they have this fault, that, when we are at feud with our next neighbours we never dare entrust to them a purpose of war. It would be strongly opposed, and inevitably revealed to some relative or friend whom it might endanger." But added the Sow with an expression of deep thankfulness, " we can impart such designs without risk of betrayal to the youngest stripling who can bear an axe."

Who can marry.

43. Marriage can take place only betwixt members of different Tribes, and not even with strangers who have been long adopted into, or domesticated with a Tribe. And a state of war or peace, appears to make little difference as to the practice of intermarriage betwixt Tribes. The people of Baramootah and of Burra Des in Goomsur have been at war time out of mind, and annually engage in fierce conflicts, but they intermarry every day. The women of each Tribe after a fight visit each other to condole on the loss of their nearest common relatives.

The wife older than the husband.

44. Reversing the usage which prevails amongst all people, of whom I have ever heard, boys of from 10 to 12 years of age amongst the Khonds, are married to girls of 15 or 16. The arrangement is of course completed by the parents of the parties. The father of the bridegroom pays 20 or 30 lives to the father of the bride, and the marriage is at once thus solemnized.

45. The father of the boy with his family and friends bear a quantity of rice and liquor in procession to the house of the parents of the girl. The priest tastes the bowl, and pours out a libation to the Gods, when the parents of the parties join hands and declare that the contract shall be completed. All present then partake of the prepared cheer.

46. An entertainment to which both families contribute equally is then prepared either at the dwelling of the bride, or at some convenient place near the house of the bridegroom. To the feast, succeed dancing and song. When the night is far spent, the principals in the scene are raised by an uncle of each upon his shoulders and borne through the dance. The burdens are suddenly exchanged, and the uncle of the youth disappears with the bride. The assembly divides into two parties, the friends of the bride endeavour to arrest those of the bridegroom to cover her flight, and men, women and children mingle in mock conflict which is often carried to great lengths. Thus the semblance of forcible abduction attends the withdrawal of the bride amongst these Orissan Tribes, as it does to a great extent amongst the Hindus, and as it did amongst many nations of ancient Europe, and now does amongst the Tribes of the Caucasus.

47. The priest who had previously bound, after Hindu fashion, a yellow thread round the necks of the parties, and sprinkled their faces with turmerick

water in the shed used for beating rice, attends them homewards to rehearse a charm in case a running brook should cross their path.

48. The new wife lives with her boy husband in his father's house, occupying the same couch, and aiding his mother in domestic labours. She leads a life of retirement compared with that of an unmarried girl, abstaining from much dancing, and from the most riotous feasts. When her husband grows up he gets a house of his own, unless he is the youngest son.

49. In the superior age of the bride is seen but a proof of the supremacy of the paternal authority amongst this singular people. The parents obtain the wives of their sons during the years of their boyhood very valuable domestic servants, and their selections are avowedly made with a view to utility in this character.

50. Notwithstanding the payment which is made by the father of the bridegroom, I think it very doubtful if the wife can be correctly considered the property of the husband.

The wife is not the property of the husband.

51. A Khoond wife, if childless, has a right to quit her husband at any time, and even if pregnant within six months after her marriage, the consideration paid by the husband to her father being in either case returned. And it appears, that a wife who chooses to retire to her father's house can in no case be forcibly reclaimed.

52. Marriage is *ipso facto* dissolved upon the discovery of a wife by the husband in adultery; and generally, when her guilt is indisputably established by other evidence. And a wife who has either voluntarily, or in consequence of such conviction, parted from her husband, cannot again contract marriage.

53. A man may, with the permission of his wife, but not otherwise, contract a second marriage, or retain a concubine during her life, and neither practice is unusual.

Polygamy and concubinage.

54. Concubinage is not reckoned, in any degree disgraceful, fathers of respectable families allowing their daughter to contract this connection.

55. The children of a concubine are in some Districts said to be of inferior rank in the family circle, and to inherit but a half share of the paternal property. In others however, they are in every respect, on a footing of equality with the children of marriage. An unmarried woman is not considered disgraced by the birth of a natural child, but no one will marry her if acquainted with the circumstance.

56. The marriage tie is said to be in general well observed among the Khonds. Although the summary infliction of the punishment of adultery is not a rare occurrence in any Tribe.

Observance of marriage.

57. It is familiarly said, that when field labour presses, a Khond wife in spite of remonstrances, binds her newly born babe round her waist and accom-

panies her husband to his toil. Khond woman upon ordinary occasions of festivity only taste the liquor cup, and habitual intoxication the great vice of the other sex, is in them uncommon and held infamous.

Drunkenness disgraceful.

58. Passing through the Districts of Moondagaum and Hodzoghoro at a season of periodical intoxication, the blowing of the mowi flower, of which the favorite Khond spirit is made, I found the country covered with frantic or senseless groups of men, but no women appeared in the least intoxicated.

59. Upon occasions of human sacrifice, however, the woman mingle freely and without shame, with the other sex, in the more than saturnalian license by which that rite is accompanied.

60. The wife and children serve the father of a family while he eats, then take their meal. Women for some unknown cause are never, I am informed, permitted to eat the flesh of the hog.

Births.

61. Khonds' births are celebrated on the seventh day after the event, by a feast given to the priest and to the whole village. To determine the best name for the child, the priest drops grains of rice into a cup of water naming with each grain a deceased ancestor. He pronounces, from the movements of the seed in the fluid, and from observations made on the person of the infant, which of his progenitors has reappeared in him, and he generally, but not uniformly, receives the name of that ancestor.

Deaths.

62. On the death of the Patriarch of a District, the event is every where proclaimed by the beating of gongs and drums, where the Abbayas and heads of society assemble from every quarter. The body is placed on a high funeral pile. A large bag of grain is laid close by upon the ground, and in it is planted a high staff bearing a flag. Over the grain are piled all the personal effects, as the cloths, arms, and eating and drinking vessels of the deceased Chief. The pile is then fired, and his family and the people of the hamlet dance, a dance peculiar to this occasion around the flag staff until it is consumed.

63. The property which is thus exposed, besides much of the live stock of the Patriarch, is distributed among the Abbayas of branches of the Tribe. The priest is usually present, but takes no part in the ceremonial, he may not touch a dead body. The dance around the flag staff is continued at intervals from the time of firing the pile until the tenth day, when there is a concourse of people from all quarters proportioned to the importance and the fame of the deceased Chief.

64. An assembly of the Tribe or District is now held, at which the heir of the late Patriarch is acknowledged, in the manner which has been already described.

65. On the death of private person his body is burnt on a pile with no ceremony, save a drinking feast, which is given to the inhabitants of the hamlets on the tenth day—every village has a separate burning ground.

SECTION IV.

USAGES OF WAR. CONVIVIAL HABITS. HABITATIONS. DRESS AND MEDICINES. LANGUAGE.

Physical character. Sacrifice and dress before battle. Arms. Character of feasts. Clothing. Habitations.

66. The Khonds are fitted by physical constitution to undergo the severest exertions, and to endure every form of privation: Their height is of about of the average standard of Hindus of the peninsula. Their forms are characterized by strength and symmetery. The muscles of the limbs and body are clean and boldly developed. The skin is clear and glossy, its colour ranging from a light bamboo to a deep copper shade, the heel is in a line with the back of the leg, the foot is somewhat larger than that of the Hindu, and the instep not highly arched, although the Khond nevertheless has extraordinary speed of foot. The forehead is full and expanded. The cheek bones are high and rather prominent, the nose is seldom, though occasionally, arched, and is generally broad at the point. The lips are full but not thick; the mouth is rather large. The whole physiognomy is generally indicative of intelligence and determination, blended with good humour. Physical character.

67. The Khonds are highly distinguished for personal courage, and never ask nor give quarter. They prepare for battle, if with an enemy of a different race, and on some occasions if, of a different tribe, by recording a vow of human sacrifice, in case of success, to the Earth God, and by propitiating Laha Pennoo, the God of Arms, both in his grove and on the field by the blood of goats and fowls, as will hereafter be described. The priest, who in no case bears arms, gives the signal to engage after the latter offering, by flourishing an axe in the air, and shouting encouragement to defiance.

68. The Khonds adorn themselves for battle, like most rude nations, as for a feast. They carefully trim their hair, plaiting it in a flat circle on the right side of the head, where it is fastened by a iron pin, and adorned with a plume of feathers, and bound with a thread of scarlet cloth when procurable.

69. I received from an eye witness the following description of a flight which took place betwixt the hostile tribes of Bora Mootah and Bora Des in Goomsur.

70. At about 12 o'clock in the day, the people of Bora Des began to advance in a mass across the Salki river, the boundary between the Districts, into the plain of Courmingia where a much smaller force was arrayed to oppose them. The combatants were protected from the neck to the loins by skins, and cloth was wound their legs down to the heel, but the arms quite bare. Round the heads of many too, cloth was wound, and, for distinction the people of Bora Mootah wore peacock's feathers in their hair, while those of Bora Des had of cock's tail plumes. They advanced with horns blowing, and gongs beat when they passed a village. The women followed behind carrying pots of water and food for refreshments, and the old men who were past bearing arms where there, giving advice and encourage-

ment. As the adverse parties approached, showers of stones, handed by the women, flew from slings from either side, and when they came within range, arrows came in flights, and many fell back wounded. At length single combats sprung up betwixt individuals who advanced before the rest, and when the first man fell, all rushed to dip their axes in his blood, and hacked the body to pieces. The first man who himself unwounded slew his opponent, struck off his right arm and rushed with it to the priest in the rear, who bore it off as an offering to Loha Pennoo in his grove. The right arms of the rest who fell were cut off in like manner, and heaped in the rear, beside the women, and to them the wounded were carried for care, and the fatigued men constantly retired for water. The conflict was at length general. All were engaged hand to hand, and now fought fiercely, now paused by common consent for a moment's breathing. In the end the men of Bora Des, although superior in numbers, began to give way, and before four o'clock they were driven across the Salki, leaving sixty men dead on the field, while the killed on the side of Bora Mootah did not exceed thirty. And from the entire ignorance of the Khonds of the simplest healing processes, at least an equal number of the wounded died after the battle. The right hands of the slain were hung up by both parties on the trees of the villages and the dead were carried off to be burned.

The people of Bora Des the next morning flung a piece of bloody cloth on the field of battle, a challenge to renew the conflict, which was quickly accepted, and so the contest was kept for three days.

Arms.

71. The arms of the Khonds are a light, long handed with a blade very curiously curved, the bow and arrow, and the sling—no shields are used. The axe is used with both hands, to strike, and guard, its handle being for the latter purpose partly defended by brass plates and wire.

72. The Khond is peculiarly dexterous in a species of ricochet shot with the bow, which it is difficult for a man to avoid: bending down, he makes his shaft fly, it is said, so as to strike the ground with its heel, at a short distance from its object, which it strikes in rising below the line of vision.

Character of feasts.

73. The feasts of the Khonds do not bear the *exclusively* sensual character which distinguishes those of many rude nations. The women partake in every form of social enjoyment but share sparingly in the liquor cup, and extemporary songs or recitations, and dancing in which the married and unmarried of both sexes join, are the accompaniments of every entertainment.

74. Still every family festival is a night long debauch which often leads to gross excess, and the guests being armed to sanguinary brawls.

Clothing.

75. The clothing of the Khonds consists of a single piece of coarse cloth, either white or chequered, from twelve to twenty cubits in length, which is in some Districts girt round the loins with its extremities flowing loose behind, and in others wrapped round the waist, and thrown across the chest something in the Hindu fashion. The women wear cloths of the same material, wound round the

waist, and brought over the shoulders. They in some Districts, wear brass armlets and anklets, and small nose and ear ornaments of gold and silver.

76. The Khonds' villages are in general beautifully situated, either by a clump of trees, or at the bases of the wooded hills, or on the knolls of the vallies slightly raised above the level of irrigation. In the Southern Districts, they consist of two rows of houses, slightly curved so as to form a broad street, which is closed at each end by a strong wooden barrier gate. Habitations.

77. In the Northern tracts, they are built after no regular plan like Hindu villages. In founding a village, the first act is to plant a Simli or great cotton tree, consecrated to the Village Deity in the centre of the site, where the house of the Abbaya is placed. The Panwa lives at either end of the village, his dwelling being marked by the pegs used for weaving, before the door. The site of a village is determined by the priest after carefully consulting the will of the God. Each man builds his own house, and the Southern Districts the walls are formed exclusively of planks placed edgewise as in a ship, the roofs being thatched. When a village begins to decay, it is not repaired, but a new one is built on a different site, and none of the old materials are used,—a Khond village lasts on a average about 14 years, but its locality is readily changed on account of other causes, besides decay, upon the slightest suspicion that the site has become unlucky from the occurrence of an unusual number of deaths, from the loss of stock, &c. the priest is put in requisition and a new hamlet is constructed.

78. The Khonds use no medicine of any sort. To wounds they apply the earth of an ant hill made into a warm mud, or a poultice of millet. They also apply, in extreme cases the actual, cautery to the belly, using a hot sickle over a wetted cloth. They are very subject to fever, and apparently to inflammation of the bowels from excessive drinking. They are often swept off in numbers by small pox and many are blind. The women suffer little or nothing in child bearing, and nurse their children only six months. Medicines.

79. Of the constitution or the grammar of the language of the Khonds, I can give no distinct account, a considerable number of its words are said to be common to the Tamul and Teloogoo languages. Its construction and inflexions appear to be regular and simple. It has more than one distinct dialect, the people of Gooldee and Degee are scarcely intelligible to the Tribes of Katingia, Godapoor and Bodoghoro, and they in consequence do not intermarry. Language.

80. Finally the distinguishing qualities of the character of the Khonds appear to be these. A passionate love of liberty, devotion to chiefs, and unconquerable resolution. They are besides faithful to friends, brave, hospitable and laborious. Their vices upon the other hand are, the indulgence of revenge, and occasionally of brutal passion. Drunkenness is universal—the habit of plunder exists in one or two small Districts alone.

PART VI.

Of the Religion of the Khonds.

1. The difficulty, under any circumstances, of ascertaining and describing with accuracy from oral statements, the opinions, feelings, and sentiments which constitute a system of religion is sufficiently apparent.

2. But with respect to an account of the superstition of the Khonds, it is necessary to keep distinctly in view, that there exists an important source of error arising from their stage of intellectual advancement, in addition to that which is incidental to the process of fixing in exact language a body of traditional ideas.

3. As has been stated above, the fundamental ideas of this rude system of faith are alone distinctly determined in the minds of the best informed of its professors—all besides is vague, fluctuating and uncertain. Hence I have found it impossible to realize in a clear and comprehensive picture, its fainter and less definite features, without heightening, in a slight degree, their distinctness and their relief. And the subject from the somewhat undue prominence which is thus given to details, has necessarily acquired, as a whole, a semblance of completeness, regularity, and system which does not strictly belong to it.

4. I propose, 1st, to consider this superstition as it is in itself, to state its leading ideas in immediate reference to its several divinities.

2dly. To describe its priestly institutions.

3rdly. To notice the influence which it exerts upon society.

SECTION I.

Of the Doctrines of the Khond Religion.

Of the Fundamental ideas of the Religion of the Khonds.

Fundamental ideas of the Khond superstition analogous to those of other races at a similar stage of mental advancement. Two classes of Native Divinities. One Hindu Divinity.

5. The religion of the Khonds in its principles, its institutions, and its influences, generally resembles the systems of superstition which have been established amongst mankind at the same stage of intellectual progress throughout the world.

6. Its divinities arise, first, from the deification of the powers which are believed to animate and to control the sensible forms of the universe, from which these powers are not yet discriminated by name; and secondly, from the adoration of the divine energy, as it is vaguely associated with abstract ideas, predominating sentiments and local objects.

7. In addition to their divinities of native origin, the portion of this people to which these observations refer, has adopted, under several of her appellations, Kali the Sacti, active energy and consort of Siva, the reproducer, who is worshipped by the Hindus of the surrounding portions of Orissa.

8. The Khond Deities may be conveniently divided into two classes, the first comprehending those which are universally acknowledged, the second, the local divinities.

9. In the first class are—

1. Bera Pennoo, or the Earth God.
2. Bella Pennoo, the Sun God, and Danzoo Pennoo, the Moon God. Deities generally acknowledged.
3. Sunde Pennoo, the God of Limits.
4. Soha Pennoo, the Iron God, or God of Arms.
5. Joogah Pennoo, the God of Small Pox.
6. Nadzoo Pennoo, or the Village Deity; the universal genius loci.
7. "Sora Pennoo," the Hill God, "Jori Pennoo," the God of Streams, and "Gossa Pennoo," the Forest God.
8. Moonda Pennoo, the Tank God.
9. Soogoo Pennoo, or Sidrojoo Pennoo, the God of Fountains.
10. Pidzoo Pennoo, the God of Rain.
11. Pilamoo Pennoo, the God of Hunting.
12. God of Births.

10. In the second class are—

1. Peetabuldee.
2. Bandri Pennoo.
3. Bahmun Pennoo. Social Deities.
4. Bahmoondi Pennoo.
5. Doongurry Pennoo.
6. Singa Pennoo.
7. Dommosinghiani.
8. Potterghor.
9. Pinjai.
10. Kunkuli.
11. Bulinda Silenda.

11. There remains the Hindu Goddess, Parvati, or Kali, worshipped by the Khonds under her names, Budramalloo, Booero and Komeswari. Of these Deities in their order. Hindu Goddess.

OF THE KHOND DIVINITIES GENERALLY ACKNOWLEDGED.

1.—Bera Pennoo, or the Earth God, in Orissan, Bloomi Devita.

Bera Pennoo, or the Earth God, worshipped under two characters. Attributes of his comprehensive character. Attributes as the divinity presiding over the powers of Bera Pennoo, or the Earth God.

nature. Institution of the rite of human sacrifice. Occasions of sacrifice. Public sacrifices. Each crop requires blood. Private sacrifices. Number of victims. The victims how procured. Acceptable victims must be bought. Occasionally married. Condition of the children of victims. Father and child not sacrificed in the same District. Escape of a victim. The rite lasts three days. The Meria grove and stream. The place of sacrifice. The sacrifice.

12. Bera Pennoo, or the Earth God, appears to be worshipped under two distinct characters, which, however, when clearly conceived, are seldom separately contemplated by his trembling votaries. He is regarded, first, as the supreme power; and secondly, as the Deity who presides over the productive energies of nature;—the two-fold aspect under which the sun, or the regent of the solar orb, was adored in the primitive Hindu Mythology.

13. The attributes of the Earth God in his comprehensive character, as the supreme or greatest power, are vague, confused, and perplexed; making up but a dim, barren abstraction in the minds of men incapable of forming ideas of power not immediately derived from the sphere of their sensible experience.

14. In this character he appears to receive distinct worship in one case only. When a Khond Tribe engages in war with enemies of another race, his awful name is invoked, and vows of sacrifice are recorded in case of success. His nature is purely malevolent, but his practical malignity towards man, is generally referred to his secondary character. He does not seem to interfere with the independent actions of the other Deities in their respective spheres, and he is no where peculiarly present.

15. As the divinity who presides over the operations of nature, the character and the functions of the Earth God are defined with a considerable degree of distinctness. They reflect, generally, the leading wants and fears of an agricultural population. He rules the order of the seasons, and sends the periodical rains. Upon him depend the fecundity of the soil, and the growth of all rural produce, the preservation of the patriarchal houses, the health and increase of the population, and in an especial manner, the safety of flocks and herds and their attendants.

Institution of rite of sacrifice.

16. The following tradition contains the only revelation relative to this Deity, which is received by his worshippers.

17. "The Earth," say the Khonds, "was originally a crude and unstable mass unfit for cultivation, and for the convenient habitation of man. The Earth God said, 'Let human blood be spilt before me!' and a child was sacrificed. The soil became forthwith firm and productive, and the Deity ordained that man should repeat the rite and live."

18. Thus the Khond enjoys the ordinary bounty of nature, on condition of deprecating by the ceaseless effusion of human blood the malignity of the power by which it's functions are controlled. This is the foundation, and in one point of view the sum of his religion.

19. The occasions and the modes of worship of the Earth God are regulated by usages which vary in every District—I shall describe those which prevail in a considerable portion of the Maliahs of Boad and of Goomsur. Occasions of sacrifice.

20. It has been stated in a former section, that contribution to the support of the ceremonial of human sacrifice,—of the rite which is the public religion is an indispensable condition of association in a Khond Tribe: and the burden appears to be distributed without difficulty in each Village, by no fixed rule, according to the means and the dispositions of individuals.

21. Sacrifices to the Earth God are either public or private—the former are offered by a Tribe, a subdivision, or a Village, the latter by individuals who are generally prompted by the immediate apprehension of the wrath of the divinity.

22. The considerations upon which the performance of public sacrifice depends, appear to be generally these.

1st. It is considered necessary that every farm should share the blood of a human victim at the time when each of it's principal crops is laid down, and particular anxiety is felt for the fulfilment of the rite in the case of the more valuable products, rice, turmeric, and mustard.

23. A Harvest oblation is deemed scarcely less necessary than the spring sacrifice; and it is considered in the last degree desirable that several offerings, according to the promise of the year should intervene betwixt them. During the hot months, when agricultural labours are nearly suspended, what may be termed cereal offerings, are not made. In some Districts, the time of new moon is always selected for these sacrifices, in others this period is not regarded.

24. Should the health of the society be affected in an extraordinary degree, or should its flocks or herds suffer from disease, or from the ravages of wild beasts, public expiations to the Earth God must be performed.

25. I have already stated in what degree the patriarchal office is connected with religious feelings; and that, practically, the fortunes of the Abbaya are as the chief index of the disposition of the Deity towards the portion of society over which he presides. Hence the failure of his crops, the loss of his farm stock, and, more especially, sickness or death in his household, are regarded as tokens of coming wrath which cannot be too speedily averted.

26. All arrangements connected with the ceremony of sacrifice are conducted by the Patriarch in concert with the priest. The divine will is in every case declared by the latter as it is communicated to him in visions; and he may demand a victim at any time, even when no visible signs of divine displeasure appear.

27. The public sacrifices to the Earth God, then, appear to be either cereal offerings, health offerings, or offerings on account of the patriarchal families.

Private sacrifices.

28. Private atonements are deemed necessary when any extraordinary calamity marks the anger of the Deity towards a particular house; as, for example, when a child watching a flock perishes by a tiger, the form which is assumed by the Earth God for purposes of wrath. Then the parents hasten to the priest, conduct him to their dwelling and dash vessels of cold water over him. When seated in his wet garments, a cup of water is placed before him into which he dips his fingers thrice, smells them, sneezes, and is filled with the God and speaks wildly in his name.

29. He of course refers the visitation to the neglected worship of the dread Deity and generally demands an immediate victim. If this requisition cannot be complied with, a goat is led to the place of sacrifice where it's ear is cut off and cast bleeding upon the earth, a pledge which must be redeemed by human blood, at whatever cost within the year.

30. In one District in the Jaypore Zemindary which I have not visited, blood is drawn from the ear of another child of the afflicted family who becomes pledged to sacrifice if a substitute cannot be provided. I have never however heard on good authority of any instance of the immolation of a Khond *in the Districts* which I have visited.

Number of victims.

31. It thus appears that the number of sacrifices in a Khond District depends upon circumstances so numerous and so variable that it is scarcely possible to form an estimate in any case of their annual average. In the valley of Bavogootza, two miles long and less than three quarters of a mile in breadth, I discovered seven victims whose immolation had been prevented by the vicinity of our troops, but it was to take place immediately upon my departure.

I proceed to describe the rite itself—

Victims how procured.

32. Victims in the Khond language "Merias," are every where procured by the Panwas, the class of Hindus, whose duties in each village have been already noticed. They purchase them without difficulty upon false pretences or kiduap them from the poorer classes of Hindus in the low country, either to the order of the Abbayas or priests or upon speculation. When brought up the mountains their price is determined by the demand varying at from fifty to a hundred lives,* a few being always, if possible, kept in reserve in each District to meet sudden demands for atonement.

* A sheep, cow, pig, fowl, &c is a life, vide part V. para. 13.

Acceptable victims.

33. Victims of either sex are equally acceptable to the Earth God, children whose age precludes a knowledge of their situation being for convenience sake, preferred. Brahmins who have assumed the brahminical thread (being perhaps regarded as already consecrated to the Deity) and Khonds are held to be unacceptable offerings, but the word of the procurer is the only guarantee of fitness in these respects which is required.

Must be bought.

34. It is a highly characteristic feature of these religion, pregnant with important consequences, that every victim, with the single exception above noticed, must be bought by the Khonds with a price, an unbought life being an abomination to the Deity.

35. The Meria is brought blind-folded to the village by the procurer, and is lodged in the house of the Abbaya in fetters if grown up, at perfect liberty if a child. He is regarded during life as a consecrated being, and if at large, is eagerly welcomed at every threshold.

36. Victims are not unfrequently permitted to attain years of maturity in ignorance of their situation, although how this ignorance can be maintained it is difficult to understand, and should one under such circumstances have intercourse with the wife or the daughter of a Khond, thankfulness is expressed to the Deity for the distinction.

37. To a Meria youth who thus grows up, a wife of one of the Hindu castes upon the mountains is generally given. Farm stock and land are presented to him, and should a family be the result, it is held to be born to the fearful condition of the sire. The sacrifice of lives bound to existence by these ties is often foregone, but should the dread divinity require atonements not easy to be afforded, the victim-father with all his children, is dragged, without hesitation, to the altars. It is a rule, however, that persons who stand in the relation of direct descent shall not be immolated in the same district, and this is so rigidly observed, that when a victim is thought in any degree to resemble a former mature sacrifice, he is always, out of precaution, either resold or exchanged. And this is, I presume, to avoid the risk of sacrificing, according to the ideas of the Khonds noticed above, the same life twice to the divinity. Occasionally married,

38. In the time of Kooli Dora Bissye of Goomsur, uncle of the present Dora Bissye, and of the class of Benniah Khonds, which has generally foregone the practice of this rite, a victim who had been permitted to attain manhood, was led out to sacrifice in the District of Rodungiah. The preliminary ceremonies had been gone through, and an intoxicated crowd expected their consummation, when the fettered youth said to the Abbaya, "In suffering this death I become, as it were, a God, and I do not resist my fate, unbind me and let me partake with you in the joy of the festival." The Abbaya consented and unbound him, and the young man called for a bowl and drank, and the crowd contended fiercely for the remains of the liquor which his lips had consecrated. He then danced and sang amid the throng, until the sacrifice could be no longer delayed, when he requested of the Abbaya to lend his axe and his bow, that he might once more join his companions armed, like a free man, in the dance. He received the weapons, and when the Abbaya was busied with the priest in preparing for the last rite, the youth approached him in the dance, and clove his skull at a blow. He then dashed across the Salki, a deep and foaming torrent, and fled down, the worshippers followed and demanded his surrender. But the Bissye contrived to cajole them until he could collect a small party of adherents, who secretly bore away the fugitive, whose descendants now live. Escape of a Victim.

39. In like manner, when the arrival of the English troops first spread confusion above the Ghauts in Goomsur, many victims sought and found protection at the hands of the present Dora Bissye.

40. From these festivals of sacrifice no one is excluded, and at them all feuds are forgotten.

41. They are generally attended by a large concourse of people of both sexes, and continue for three days, which are passed in the indulgence of every form of gross excess in more than saturnalian license.

The rite lasts three days.

42. The first day and night are spent exclusively in drinking, feasting, and obscene riot. Upon the second morning the victim who has fasted from the preceding evening is carefully washed, dressed in a new garment, and led forth from the village in solemn procession with music and dancing.

The Meria Grove and Stream.

43. The Meria grove, a clump of deep and shadowy forest trees, in which the Mango, the Bur, the Saul, and the Peepul generally prevail, usually stands at a short distance from the hamlet, by a rivulet which is called the Meria stream. It is kept sacred from the axe, and is avoided by the Khond as haunted ground; my followers were always warned to abstain from seeking shelter within its awful shades. In its centre, upon the day of sacrifice, an upright stake is fixed, and generally between twoplants of the Sunkissar or Buzzur dauti shrub, the victim is seated at its foot, bound back to it by the priest. He is then anointed with oil, ghee, and turmeric, and adorned with flowers, and a species of reverence which it is not easy to distinguish from adoration, is paid to him throughout the day. And there is now infinite contention to obtain the slightest relic of his person ; a particle of the turmeric paste with which he is smeared, or a drop of his spittle, being esteemed, especially, by the women, of supreme virtue. In some districts, instead of being thus bound in a grove, the victim is exposed in, or near the village, upon a couch, after being led in procession around the place of sacrifice. And in some parts of Goomsur where this practice prevails, small rude images of beasts and birds in clay are made in great numbers of this festival and stuck on poles, a practice of the origin or meaning of which I have been able to obtain no satisfactory explanation.

44. Upon the third morning the victim is refreshed with a little milk and palm sago, while the licentious feast which has scarcely been intermitted during the night, is loudly renewed. About noon, these orgies terminate, and the assemblage issues forth with stunning shouts, and pealing music, to consummate the sacrifice.

45. As the victim must not suffer bound, nor on the other hand, exhibit any shew of resistance, the bones of his arms, and if necessary, those of his legs, are now broken in several places.

The place of sacrifice.

46. The acceptable place of sacrifice has been discovered the previous night, by persons sent out for this purpose, into the fields of the village, or of the private oblator. The ground is probed in the dark with long sticks, and the first deep chink that is pierced is considered the spot indicated by the Earth God. The rod is left standing in the earth, and in the morning four large posts are set up around it

The sacrifice.

47. The priest assisted by the Abbaya, and by one or two of the elders of the village, now takes the branch of a green tree which is cleft a distance of several feet down the centre. They insert the victim within the rift, fitting it in some districts to his chest, in others, to his throat. Cords are then twisted round the open extremity of the stake, which the priest, aided by his assistants, strives with his whole

force to close. He then wounds the victim slightly with his axe, when the crowd throws itself upon the sacrifice, and exclaiming " we bought you with a price, and no sin rests on us?" strips the flesh from the bones.

48. Each man bears his bloody shreds to his fields and from thence returns straight home; and for three days after the sacrifice, the inhabitants of the village which afforded it remain dumb, communicating with each other only by signs, and remaining unvisited by strangers. At the end of this time, a buffaloe is slaughtered at the place of sacrifice, when tongues are loosened.

49. Such is one of the endless variety of modes in which human life is offered up by the Khonds.

A. Neither the Khonds of Degee nor those of Goldee attached to the Zemindary of Koradah, nor those of Kotingea or of Borogoda connected with Chinna Kimedy, offer human sacrifices to the Earth God. A tree is substituted for the Meriah, and each village performs this worship separately, there being no licentious concourse of the people of the Tribe. The first day is passed in feasting as has been described above. On the second, the priest and elders go into the jungle, and choose a young tree which they cut down, and bring away a portion of it about the height of a man. They then either fix it at once in the earth in the appointed place, or take it into the village to be brought forth again in procession like a human victim. On the third day, all come forth men, women and children. A bull or a pig is sacrificed. Its legs being human-strung as the limbs of the Meriah are broken, while its blood is allowed to mingle with a heap of rice placed at the foot of the stake. Now the priest strikes the sacred tree with his axe and nearly all present go through this form, when the bloody rice is carried off and deposited in the fields like the flesh of the human sacrifice. The people of Degee do not eat with those who offer Meriahs, although these do not object to food cooked by them; but this difference in religious practice does not prevent intermarriages.

2.—Bella Pennoo, the Sun God, and Danzoo Pennoo, the Moon God.

50. The Sun and the Moon are universally recognized as Deities by the Khonds, but no ceremonial worship is addressed to either. They are acknowledged, by a simple reverence, which is paid to them when visible, upon every occasion of public solemnity whether religious or not.

Bella Penno, the Sun God, and Danzoo Pennoo, the Moon God.

3.—Sundi Pennoo, the God of Limits.

Adored by human victims on boundaries. Other victims.

51. It is easy to understand, that amongst clusters of jealous tribes which depend entirely upon the soil, a God of Limits should be universally acknowledged. He is apparently to be regarded as a manifestation of the Earth God, as it may be observed the same power in the Roman mythology, before the coming of Terminus was one with Jupiter. He is adored by the same rite as the great divinity; but besides the blood of human victims, that of buffaloes and of goats is

Sundi Pennoo, the God of Limits.

acceptable to him. Particular points upon the boundaries of districts, fixed by ancient usage, and generally upon the highways are his altars; and these demand, each, an annual victim, who is either an unsuspecting traveller struck down by his priests, or a sacrifice provided by purchase, as for the Earth God.

52. On the boundary between Ruttabarri and Oogdoor on the Kattigootza-ghaut, and on that of the same district on the side of Bulscoopa, this rite is never omitted. Upon the latter, where, it is marked by some low barricades a mile from Sooroodoocoopa, the bones of a late victim whitened when I passed. On the ghaut between Kooradicottah and Borogootza, there is a similar place of sacrifice marked by a turmeric-smeared stone, which stands beneath a spreading mango tree, and is called "Lutchmiputter" by the trembling Hindu. On the boundary between North Atcombo and Boad is also a well known place of sacrifice distinguished by a heap of stones. "Sundi" is the Khond and the Orissan word for "boundary."

4.—Loha Pennoo, the God of Arms.

His Symbol. When invoked. Victims.

Loha Pennoo, the God of Arms.

53. The God of Arms has in every Khond village, at least in the Southern districts, a grove sacred from the axe, in the centre of which, beneath a spreading tree, his symbol is buried—a piece of iron, about two cubits in length, and to no Khond God is worship more assiduously or devoutly paid.

54. When war is resolved upon, the priest accompanied by a few of the leading elders, while women and children abhorred by this God, are carefully kept at a distance, enters his grove. He sacrifices a young chicken, letting the blood sink into the earth over the symbol, then pours out a libation of palm toddy, and then presents an addled egg and some rice, all the while invoking the presence of the Deity, saying "our youth are going out to fight, go thou out before them." The priest then divides some rice into a number of small heaps, and offers one to Bera Pennoo and to each of the other Deities whom he thinks proper to propitiate. He then leaves the grove accompanied, it is believed, by the Deity, if propitious. On the outside there await him the whole youth of the tribes completely armed. He heaps their arms with much solemnity in a pile, by a stream, and sprinkles them with water with a handful of long grass. He then calls loudly upon Loha Pennoo, and upon Bera Pennoo (if it is not a case of family feud,) and on the war Gods of the hills, and on all the other Gods. Loha Pennoo now possesses the priest, who becomes bacchant, raving wildly with hair cast loose and shouting in phrenzy, while all shout with him. He then seizes a handful of the arms, points towards the hostile quarter, and delivers them to those nearest, who rush off, followed by the rest as they can snatch weapons from the heap. They make straight for the nearest of their enemy's villages, and attack any of the inhabitants whom they find in the fields, but no one met upon the road—for there even while a conflict is going on any one is safe. If they find no one in the fields, they go up to the tree next village and wound it with an axe. When the people thus attacked have taken the alarm, they shout defiance from every village and both sides give themselves up to preparations for

battle on the morrow. The priest before the battle makes a fresh offering to Loha Pennoo in the field and gives the signal to engage. He himself waits in the rear until some warrior himself unwounded, can bring the right arm of a slain, for with which trophy they both rush to the grove of Loha Pennoo, where the priest presents it to the God with prayers that he will make the axes of the tribe more sharp and their arrows more sure.

55. Success in arms is carefully ascribed in every case to the immediate interposition of the Loha Pennoo—never to personal valour.

It is in the power of the priest upon any occasion to prevent war by declaring Loha Pennoo to be unfavorable.

5.—Joogah Pennoo, the God of Small Pox.

His Offerings.

56. Joogah Pennoo, say the Khonds, "sows small pox upon mankind as men sow seed upon the earth." When a village is threatened with this dread disease, it is deserted by all save a few persons who remain to offer the blood of buffaloes, hogs, and sheep, to the destroying power. The inhabitants of the neighbouring hamlets attempt to prevent his approach by planting thorns in the path which lead towards the infected place.

Joogah Pennoo: the God of Small Pox.

6.—Nadzoo Pennoo, the Village God.

His functions, victims and Priest.

57. The Nadzoo Pennoo, or Village God, is the guardian Deity of every hamlet. These universal lares are the great objects of the domestic and familiar worship of the Khonds. The ruin or prosperity of villages is in their power. Their aid is implored as patrons in every undertaking—vows are made and registered to them in sickness: and the Village Deity is especially invoked as Lucina. In Orissa and Tellingana, the rural Gods who bear the same designation are Hindu Gods localized, and assumed as patron Deities, but the Nadzoo Pennoo of the Khonds appears to be a local influence quite distinct from the greater divinities.

Nadzoo Pennoo, the Village God.

His functions.

58. This God is familiarly approached by all at his shrine, which is simply marked by a stone placed under the cotton tree, which is planted in the centre of every village on its foundation—sheep, fowls, and pigs, with grains and fruit, are his offerings. The Village Abbaya is his priest, but any one may minister for himself at his altar. "Nadzoo" is the Orissan word for a village.

7.—"Soro Pennoo," the Hill God, "Jori Pennoo," the God of Streams, and "Gossa Pennoo," the Forest God.

59. Every hill and knoll in the Khond country has a name, and a divinity, who is called "Soro Pennoo," but to whom no formal worship is addressed. "Jori Pennoo" is the God of Streams, but has in like manner no peculiar rites. "Gossa

Soro Pennoo, the Hill God.

"Jori Pennoo," the God of Streams.

" Gossa Pennoo," the Forest God.

Pennoo," the Forest God, has a locality within the limits of every village, where the following observances are paid to him, at least in the Southern Districts.

60. That timber may never be wanting in case of accidents from fire or from enemies, a considerable grove, generally of saul, is uniformly dedicated by every village to Gossa Pennoo, and religiously preserved. It is consecrated by the priest by drawing a line round it with a bamboo split at one end, and having a fowl, an offering to the God, attached to the other. The bird is then sacrificed with the usual accompaniments of rice and an addled egg in the centre of the grove, the names of all the other Gods being invoked after that of the Sylvan Deity. The young trees of this wood are occasionally pruned, but not a twig is cut for use without the formal consent of the village, nor can the axe even then be applied before " Gossa Pennoo" has been propitiated by the sacrifice of a sheep or a hog.

8.—" Moonda Pennoo," the Tank God.

Moonda Pennoo, the Tank God.

61. The Khonds carefully collect for the purpose of irrigation, the waters of their rivulets near these sources, by rude, weak dams, called " Moonda," and they assiduously sacrifice sheep and fowls to " Moonda Pennoo" under the nearest tree, praying him to preserve these embankments.

9.—" Soogoo Pennoo," or Sidroojoo Pennoo, the God of Fountains.

Soogoo Pennoo, or Sidroojoo Pennoo, the God of Fountains.

62. The Gods of Fountains are, amongst the Khonds, objects of the most anxious and regular worship. When a spring dries up, the priest is instantly sent for by the despairing villagers, and conjured to bring back the water with promises of all that they can command. He plucks the cocoon of a silk worm from a bamboo tree, and in the dead of the night steals to some living fountain to endeavour to induce the God to transfer a portion of its waters to the deserted spring : and at the imminent risk of his life if his errand should become known to the proprietors of the waters to be wiled away.

63. The Kottagottaroo remains a long time alone over these muttering incantations, by which he generally prevails with " Soogoo Pennoo." He then fills the cocoon from the spring, and returns to the dry fountain, repeating charms as he goes, while it is believed a stream of water follows his footsteps under ground. The Abbaya, with a party of old men who have fasted the preceding day (the presence of women being here peculiarly fatal, while that of youths is also interdicted) awaits his return at the deserted well. Its basin is now cleared out and the cocoon cup of water is placed in it. The priest then sacrifices a sheep or a hog to Soogoo Pennoo, who either immediately renews the spring, or gives signs of satisfaction which are always followed by its re-appearance in a day or two.

10.—Pidza Pennoo, the God of Rain.

Pidza Pennoo, the God of Rain.

64. When there is a failure of rains, a whole tribe generally meets to invoke " Pidza Pennoo." Quarrels are now forgotten or suspended, and all go forth, men, women and children, accompanied by the loudest music ; the men shouting and

capering madly in the circles. The God of Showers is sought at some old appointed tree or rock, while some keep up the dance without remission, others strip and cook the victims, which are bullocks, sheep or hogs, and which are sacrificed with invocations by the Kottagottaroo. He first eats with the old men, who have fasted from the preceding day. Then the young men eat, and finally the women and children who have sat by, receive their share.

Pilamoo Pennoo, the God of Hunting.

65. When a hunting party is formed the Khonds always require the priest to propitiate to the God of Chace—The huntsmen. He piles their weapons by a rivulet, sprinkles water over their well, a handful of long grass, and sacrifices a fowl to the God, who if propitious inspires him to indicate the direction in which the chase is to be pursued and occasionally enables him to devote so many sombre wild hog, hares, &c., to fall. A hunting party generally consists of from 30 to 50 persons, who drive and mob the game, killing it with their bow, slings and axes. That hot weather is the season for sport. The Khonds, strange to say, are unacquainted with the use of the poison for the arrows, although the neighbouring Sourahs have a poison said to be so active as soon to kill a tiger. Pilamoo Pennoo, the God of Hunting.

11.—God of Births.

66. When the birth of a child does not take place at the expected time, the priest is immediately put in requisition as on every other conceivable occasion of doubt or difficulty amongst the Khonds. He takes the woman to the place of confluence of two streams, sprinkles water over her and makes an offering to the Deity—when any animal fails in fertility the same God is appealed to. God of Births.

The Khond Local Divinities.

1. *Peetabuldee. The great Father God Peetabuldee ; His name ; where worshipped ; His shrine ; His offerings.*

67. Peetabuldee is a compound Orissan word signifying "Great Father God." This Deity is worshipped in Chokapaud, Hodzoghoro, Oogdoor, and Nowsagur, while in the western and southern Khond Districts his name is unknown. His symbol is a stone smeared with turmeric placed under a lofty forest tree where tradition generally records that a rift once marked his passage into or his emergence from the earth. Peetabuldee has a temple by a grove at Goodrisye between Gattigoodoo and Bonee. It is a shed 10 or 12 feet square, with a raised floor. Within is a low vacant mud enclosure two feet in diameter, in front stands a post to which victims are bound for sacrifice. Peetabuldee—his shrines,

68. To Peetabuldee are due two yearly offerings, one at seed time the other at harvest. They usually consist of a goat or a few fowls, with milk, turmeric, rice, ghee and incense, and buffaloes are occasionally sacrificed. The blood of the victim is partly spilt on the rice of the offering, partly allowed to sink into the soil where the rift is supposed to have existed.

2.—Bandri Pennoo.

Bandri Pennoo. His shrines appeared in a material form at Borapal. Effects of his removal.

Bandri Pennoo.

69. Bandri Pennoo enjoys great influence in the District of Nowsagur, in the Zemindary of Duspallah, where he is manifested in a material form, and has a temple. In Borogoobza he has also a shrine which is kept by Pedda Dehri, the Patriarch of the subdivision, and which is exactly similar in form to that of Peetabuldee in Goodrisye. Of this Deity, the present Majee, the Patriarch of Nowsagur, states that he manifested himself at Borapall in the form under which he is now adored there some years ago upon the occasion of his (the Majee's) marriage.

70. The God was found in the large dish of rice, which according to custom his wife's mother at that ceremony placed upon his head. Its material, I was assured, is neither gold, silver, wood, iron, stone, nor any other known substance. It is deposited in a small building under the guardianship of a Hindu priest, who is entertained for this service, and who at the time of my visit was unfortunately absent at some distance with the key.

71. The Rajah of Duspallah a few years ago carried away this sacred symbol by force, when the village of Borapall was nearly depopulated by disease and tigers. The Deity was afterwards restored and these plagues ceased. Bandri Pennoo and Peetabuldee are worshipped by similar rites.

3.—Bahmun Pennoo and Bahmoondi Pennoo.

Bahmun Pennoo and Bahmoondi Pennoo.

72. Bahmun Pennoo, apparently the Brahmin God, and Bahmoondi Pennoo of suspicious similarity in point of sound, are honored by rites similar to those paid to Peetabuldee in the District to the Eastward of the great table land, where the Khonds have perhaps been most exposed to impressions from Hinduism. The latter is also worshipped in Senteliaghur. It may be observed that tradition records the existence of a Hindu city founded by Rama on his return from Ceylon in Chokapaud, where these Deities are chiefly adored. My time unfortunately did not admit of my examining the remains of one or two Hindu temples which exist there.

5.—Dhoongurri Pennoo.

His worship.

Dhoongurri Pennoo.

73. This Deity is exclusively worshipped in the districts of Hoodzoghoro and Senteliaghur. In him the Khonds appear to adore an influence which is new to ceremonial worship, namely, the conservative principal or rather that of the status quo.

74. Upon the filling altar of Dhoongurri, a lofty mountain, the blood of victims is annually poured outbefore an immense concourse of devotees, whose single aspiration is "may we ever live as did our forefathers, and may our children hereafter live like us."

75. The greater part of the population whose predominant sentiment is thus expressed by a prayer for perpetual infancy, appeared to me under circumstances peculiarly unfavourable to minute inquiry upon any subject.

76. The Mowi-tree had just blossomed, and in the drunken festival by which its flowers are welcomed, I beheld the dreadful spectacle of the male population of an entire community, amongst which my route lay for two days, deprived of reason. But no women added degradation to the scene.

77. To Dhoongurri are sacrificed, buffaloes, goats and pigs.

Singa Pennoo.

Singa Pennoo manifested in Oogadoor. Stolen. His nature.

Singa Pennoo.

78. The God "Singa Pennoo," said the chief of Oogadoor, in which District alone he is worshipped, "rose from the Earth in the form of a piece of iron which was called "Hooma Pennoo," (the word "Huma" having no meaning in the Khond language) until the Deity revealed his true name "Singa," which is equally without meaning, to his priest in a dream. The late Rajah Joognaje of Boad, adorned the sacred symbol with a silver top, when it was stolen by an impious Khond. The thief perished miserably with a smith, his confederate, who attempted to convert the Deity into an axe. The mother of the former replaced the sacred iron, when a temple was for safety built over it."

His Character.

79. The habits of this God are destructive. The tree, under which he is placed, certainly dies. If he is laid in water it dries up. His priest cannot expect to survive in his service, the term of four years, while he cannot decline the fearful office.

80. Thus it appears that of the four rude temples, which are found in these districts, that of Bandri Pennoo at Baropall, and that of Singa Pennoo, have been recently constructed for the safe custody of symbols, which had been previously abstracted by force or stealth. A third, which is vacant, stands in Borogootza, in honor of the former God, while the fourth in Chokapaud is devoted to Peetabuldee, whose worship is almost exclusively in Hindoo Khonds. No other Khond temples, I believe, exist in Goomsur, Boad or Duspullah.

81. The Khonds appear to be as far removed from the ideas, which give rise to the temples and to idol worship from the idea of conferring or of personifying the divine presence, as were the Persian priests, who incited Xerxes to burn the temples of the Greeks on the ground of their being inconsistent with the very nature of God.

82. A moss grown rock on the hill of Koludah, in Goomsur, which bore a rude natural resemblance to a man seated on a tiger, had been, from the remotest antiquity, an object of superstitious veneration. The father of the late Rajah of Goomsur, in compliment to the Jakso-Tribe, whose former territory included Koladah, built a temple near the spot, and placed within it the image of a man and tiger of the best Hindu workmanship. The gaudy idol remained entirely unnoticed while the

Khonds continued to regard the rude natural image with the unabated reverence. In the year 1815, however, when a British force took possession of Koladah, a party of Sepoys chanced to bivouack in the temple. Their camp fire was allowed to scorch the idol, and a Musselman contemptuously pricked the nose of the tiger with his bayonet. Blood, say the Khonds, flowed from the wound, and a pestilence wasted the English camp, which proved that their divinity had transferred his presence from his ancient hill to the new Hindu shrine. Thither they declined to follow him, but the tiger rock has since ceased to be in any degree an object of religious regard.

7—Dommosinghiam. 8—Potterghor. 9—Pinjai. 10—Bulinda Silendi. 11—Kunkali.

Dommosinghiam, tutelary God of Dommosinghi. Potterghor and Pinjai, names of places. Bulinda Silendi and Kunkali unknown.

83. Dommosinghiam is simply the tutelary God of the district of Dommosinghi, and no doubt represents in accordance with all analogy, a vague sense of the dependence of the community upon the divine power. The Abbayas are his priests.

84. Potterghor and "Pinjai" are names of places (I believe of ghauts) in the tracts which the Deities so designated are recognized.

85. Bulinda Silendi and Kunkali are local Gods of the district of Punchora, with respect to whom I possess no exact information.

4—The Hindu Goddess Kali.

Hindu Goddess Kali.

86. The Khonds have adopted in addition to their native Gods, the Goddess Kali, the Chief Deity of the Hindus in this quarter of Orissa, and whom all the Zemindars recently adored, and in many cases, no doubt, still adore by the rite of human sacrifice. Her worship is every where postponed by the Khonds to that of their principal native Divinities, except perhaps, at Raneegunze, in Otcomba, where the head of the priestly branch of the chief Khonro family is her minister, and where her service is apparently combined with that of the Earth God, the offerings thus acquiring a double significance. Kali is recognized under these three names, Budwalloo, Boero, and Komeswari. Her ordinary offerings are buffaloes, goats and fowls.

87. Such are the Khond Divinities and their worship, in a part of Boad and of Goomsur, I proceed to speak of the institution of priesthood.

SECTION II.

The Khond Priesthood.

Origin. Of two Classes. 1. The Khond Priesthood. Appellations. In what respect distinguished from the Community. Magical Arts. Equality. Emoluments. 2. Hindoo priests.

Origin.

88. The Khond priesthood, like every other priesthood, lays claim to divine institution. Each Deity originally appointed ministers in every tribe by which he was recognized and the office is hereditary, descending usually but not necessarily

to eldest sons. But no exclusive privilege is transmitted by descent. The priestly office may be assumed by any one who chooses to assert a call to the service of a God; the mandate being communicated in a dream or vision, and the ministry of any Divinity, may, apparently, be laid aside at pleasure. Hence the Khond priesthood has no tendency to form a caste.

Of two classes.

89. In addition to the native priesthood, a class of Hindus, whose number is not considerable, is employed by the Khonds in the service of their Gods. The Khond priesthood conducts exclusively the worship of the Earth God, and generally that of the Deities who are universally acknowledged, while it divides with the Hindu ministers the service of the local Gods and of Kali, and apparently according to no fixed rules.

The Khond priesthood.

90. In Goomsur and the northern part of Boad the Khond name for a priest is "Koottagottaroo," or "Sorumba," in the Western Districts it is "Jackora". The Orissan appellations of "Jauni" and "Dehri" are, however, occasionally adopted; the former generally by the priests of the Earth God, the latter by those of the local Deities and Kali.

91. Every Khond village has it's priest. In some districts, as those of Oogdoor and Baramullick, the chief civil and sacerdotal offices are generally united, in others they are always distinct. But I apprehend that they were originally held in every case, if not by the same person by members of the same family.

In what respect distinguished from the community.

92. The Khond priest is separated from the rest of the community only in these respects—1st. He may not eat with laymen, nor partake of food prepared by their hands. This rule does not however extend to the liquor cup, of which he partakes freely at feasts, while a portion of uncooked flesh is reserved for him. His family does not share this restriction.

93. 2ndly. The Khond priest in no case bears arms—when war is undertaken with enemies of a different race he first invokes the Earth God as above stated and then Loha Pennoo. When the contest is between Khond Tribes, he makes an offering to the latter Deity alone, in the space which divides the combatants, and, on the completion of the rite flourishes his axe twice in the air utters shouts of defiance, and retires, while the conflict is joined.

Magical arts.

94. The Khonds, like all other people at the same stage of advancement believe in charms and incantations, but their superstition is but slightly connected with medicine. One of the chief duties of a priest however is to discover the causes of sickness, as of every other species of misfortune either in the immediate displeasure of some Deity, or of some ancestor ungratified by food and honours.

95. Upon such occasions the Kottagottaroo seats himself by the afflicted person, and taking some rice divides it into small heaps, each dedicated to a God whom he names. He then balances a sickle with a thread, places a few grains upon each end, and calls all the Gods by name. The sickle is slightly agitated. A God has come perching by the offering. The priest

declares his name and lays down the sickle. He then counts the heap of rice dedicated to that God, if odd in number the Deity is offended if even he is pleased. In the former case, the priest becomes full of the God, shakes his head frantically with dishevelled hair and utters wild incoherent sentences. The patient addresses the God in his minister, enquiring humbly the cause of his displeasure. He refers to his neglected worship, sorrow is professed and forgiveness prayed, and the sacrifices prescribed by the priest instantly performed. Deceased ancestors are invoked in the same way as Gods, and appeased by offerings of fowls, rice and liquor. The consecrated rice with the brass vessels used in these ceremonies are the perquisite of the priest.

96. The presence of the Khond priest at the marriage feast, as noticed in a preceding Section, seems to be chiefly for the prevention of injury to the parties by the magical arts of ill wishers. His office on the occasions of the birth or the naming of a child is to decide which ancestor of the family is born again. He is a guest at funeral feasts, as at all other domestic ceremonies.

Equality.

97. The members of the priesthood, in accordance with the general spirit of Khond society are of course perfectly equal in point of rank, although some degree of traditional precedence is necessarily enjoyed by the older priestly families. They have neither privileges nor endowments in any form. Their land is not tilled by the common labour as is the custom among the neighbouring Sourahs. They have an honorable place at all public and private festivals, receive as above observed, perquisites of some value at certain ceremonies, and occasional harvest offerings of good will when the Deity to whom they minister, has proved propitious.

Endowments.

Hindu priesthood.

98. The Hindu priesthood employed by the Khonds, is composed partly of the class of hereditary Civil Officers—the Bissyes, Mahalickos, Dulbehras, &c., above described ; partly of other employes, who are usually of Soodoo caste. In Chotrapaud, Kodzoghora, and Senteliliaghor, the former, as we have seen, minister to Peetabuldee. In Nowsagur some of the latter are entertained for the service of Bandri Pennoo. Hindus generally perform the worship of Kali, although a Khond Dehri discharges her rites under the name of Budrawulloo at Raneegunze of Atcombo ; and in the Western Districts, Khond priests frequently minister to her as Komeswari. These Soodoo priests are generally supported, as at Boropall in Nowsagur, by allotments of land. It is curious to mark in every collection, as in this instance, of a few priests maintained by a grant of the soil for the stated ministration of a temple, the germ of an endowed ecclesiastical corporation. Of the degree of influence enjoyed by the Khond priesthood I shall afterwards speak.

SECTION III.

Of the influence which the religion of the Khonds exerts upon society.

99. Such appear to be the leading ideas, and the priestly institutions, of the Khond superstition.

100. It is doubtful whether it may be most correctly designated, in general terms ; vague, confused theism, with a subordinate demonology, or a demonology in which the idea of a supreme power is distinctly to be traced.

101. This rude faith involves no reference to principles of morality. The neglect of prescribed ordinances is alone offensive, their observance alone pleasing to the Gods; and it presents no view relative to the future destiny of man, except that he has an imperishable spirit which animates an endless succession of human forms, and generally in the order of direct descent. Fear, the apprehension of evil, is its predominating idea. The attributes of the supreme or greatest power are purely malevolent. He is clothed in terror, and delights in vengeance, and his worshippers aspire only to deprecate his wrath, by the sacrifice of human life, which, as the costliest offering has obtained under an infinite variety of forms in the religious ceremonials of almost every race of mankind of whose superstition at an early stage of advancement we have any knowledge.

102. The Khond divinities are all confined to the limits of the earth, within it they are believed to reside, emerging and retiring at will by chinks which are occasionally discovered to their worshippers—and they all assume earthly forms at pleasure; the Earth God, for example, adopting that of the tiger as emblematic of his nature, or as convenient for purposes of wrath.

103. The priesthood of the chief God is composed exclusively of Khonds, that of the lesser divinities of both Khonds and Hindus. The ministry of all is hereditary, but no exclusive privileges are transmitted by descent,—the sacred office being open to all who may choose to construe a desire to enter it as a call from the divinity.

104. The point of development which this superstition has attained appears to be nearly that which is ascribed to the religion of Greece in the Pelasgic period, and not remote from that which is attributed to the superstition of ancient Germany.

105. In terms of the former mythology, it is the reign of Cælus and of Serra, of high and the starry signs, the Genii and the Nymphs, and the "Gods now forgotten" of Hesiod. Before the dynasties of Olympus, to which later speculations assigned a cosmological character. Before Homer and the bards conferred unity and nationality upon the perplexed mythical circles of Greece. When the primary Deities were honored in the forms of nature over which they presided, and the lesser and the derived Gods were symbolically adored in blocks of wood and stone, as were the Goddess of Sterility at Paphos, the God of Love as Thespis, and the Graces at Orchomenos.

106. If this superstition neither tends to raise the minds of its professors above the earth, nor imposes upon them any duties towards their kind, it acts, like all systems of religious belief bearing the same general character, as a strong and fruitful principle of association. Participation in the public worship, and contribution to the charges of its ceremonial are, as has been already observed, the first conditions of association in a Tribe, applicable even to strangers of a different race, and faith. And the bond of a common altar and a distinctive worship is seen to survive the blended ties springing from community of institutions, of manners, of traditions, and of language.

107. Many families who leaving isolated in the wilder tracts of the Zemindaries, or mingling in close intercourse with the Hindu population, have lost most of their distinctive ideas, habits, and sentiments, and wholly or in part, their ancient tongue, remain firmly bound to their race by the tie of religious sympathy. They visit the mountain districts periodically, to participate in the great rite ; whilst, upon the other hand, the hill tribes who have maintained their usages pure, endeavour to retain within the ancient bond of their social communion, important individuals or families (as in the case of Dora Bissye) who may tend to exchange it for that of the more civilized people, by making them involuntary partakers in their neglected sacrifices, by conveying a share of the victims to their fields.

108. The festivals of the Earth God, in fact, tend to maintain a sense of unity betwixt the Khond tribes and their sub-divisions, and amongst the whole people, in some degree analogous to that which the sacred games at Elis produced amongst the various and minutely divided population of ancient Greece.

109. The practice of human sacrifice does not appear to exert upon the character of this rude people, an influence so eminently unfavorable to humanity as that which has been attributed to it in the case of some other races of mankind.

110. Where the victims have been prisoners of war, this may be at least partially accounted for. When the Mexicans loaded the altar of their horrid Deity with slaughtered captives ; or when the Admiral of the fleet of Xerxes sacrificed upon his prow the chief of the first galley which was taken at Salamis, the indulgence of an inhuman passion at war with the first principles of society was sanctified by association with the worship of the Deity.

111. Amongst the Khonds, the sacrifice of human life is combined with the gratification of no anti-social passion, or brutalizing feeling, although it is accompanied by indulgence in the worst forms of sensual excess.

112. The rite is discharged with feelings almost purely religious, in fearful obedience to the express mandate of the terrible power whose wrath it is believed to place in abeyance. And the offerings are lives free, unforfeited, undegraded, generally in innocent childhood, belonging to a different race from the immolators, procured by persons of another faith, and acquired by scrupulous purchase which the Khonds believe to confer a perfect title. They are obtained and offered up without passion. When the axes of the crowd are raised to complete the rite, the justificatory exclamation is upon their lips "we bought you with a price."

Influence of the priesthood.

113. The Khond priesthood being separated in no respect from the community, being depressed every where throughout it, and participating upon equal grounds in all its interests and engagements, is obviously in a highly favorable situation for the acquisition of power, and its influence as a body of interpreters of the will of the Deity, as mediators betwixt him and a man, and as adepts in magical arts is, generally speaking, great.

114. When the priest is not combined with the Patriarchal office, the civil and the religious heads of Tribes, although some districts are vexed by their rivalry, generally act in concert, while the former desire to strengthen their hands as temporal rulers by the aid of superstition, the latter aim at influence through alliance with the secular authority.

115. When the place of an Abbaya whose race has become extinct is to be supplied by popular election, the community is almost uniformly guided in its choice by the Koottagottaroo, who does not omit upon such occasions to consult with vigils and fasting the will of the Deity. And when, in the public council, a priest of venerable age and character demands, in language which modulated to the time, has been employed at one period or another by the spiritual order of every faith "Will men not listen to those to whom God listens?" The appeal is rarely resisted.

PART VII.

Of Measures to be adopted towards the Mountain Khonds.

SECTION I.

The History of our Connection with the Khonds. Our Objects with respect to them.

1. I have thus endeavoured to exhibit the leading facts of the physical, the social, and the moral situation of this portion of the Khond people.

2. I proceed to enquire what practical measures should be adopted towards them,—1st, as a question of policy,—2ndly, with reference to their religion.

3. The facts of their history which are material to this enquiry appear to be briefly these.

4. These Tribes have existed from a period of the remotest antiquity, as they are seen at present, nearly isolated by manners, language, and prejudices of race from the surrounding Hindu population; while they have been until recently completely cut off by the interposed Zemindary domains, from all contact, from all relations with the successive Governments which these have acknowledged. To these Zemindaries they have been attached, individually, and in loosely coherent groups, as independent but subordinate allies.

5. The barrier by which they were thus separated from our immediate provinces was suddenly removed by our assumption of the Zemindary of Goomsur for arrears of Tribute, which was followed by the rebellion of its Rajah, in the end of the year 1835.

6. That Chief retired before a force which advanced to apprehend him, and to take possession of his Estates, into the Khond Districts above the Ghauts, which were most anciently attached to Goomsur, and there he soon after died.

7. A small body of troops then penetrated the great mountain chain for the first time to endeavour to obtain possession of his heir, of the remaining members of his family, and of his treasures.

8. The region into which it advanced was entirely unexplored. Of the Khond people we knew nothing save the name. We were ignorant of the nature of the connections, which subsisted between them and Goomsur, or the neighbouring Zemindaries. We knew nothing of their social organization, of their feelings towards the late Zemindar, or towards ourselves, of their numbers, their language, or their manners: while they could have formed no idea of the character of our power, of our views, of any of our objects.

9. A part of the mountain population was already combined against us, without any suspicion on our part, in anticipation of the course which we pursued; and was arrayed in the name of every authority which they regarded as legitimate, confirmed by the most binding religious solemnities, and in the sacred name of hospitality.

10. The dying Rajah had obtained a pledge from several of the Tribes of the plateau, given before their great divinity, to prevent in any event *the capture* of his family which had suffered treatment in the last degree dishonorable at our hands upon a former occasion when taken by Colonel Fletcher's force* in 1815.

* Col. F. divided with his officers the ladies and treasures of the Rajah and was dismissed by a Court Martial in 1817.

11. The disposition of the Khonds, at first considered amicable, was observed to tend towards hostility; upon the apprehension of these distinguished guests, but the existence of their pledge first appeared from a bold, startling, and partially successful attempt to fulfil it. They rose and overwhelmed a small detachment which (contrary to the intentions of the Commissioner) was employed to escort a portion of the family of the Zemindar by a difficult pass from the plateau to the low country, putting to death, to prevent their dishonour, seven ladies of his Zenana.

12. The Tribes which was chiefly implicated in this movement, immediately felt the weight of our vengeance. But the extreme sickliness of the advancing season soon after compelled us to suspend active operations.

13. At the end of the rains, a large and nearly fresh force of every arm was assembled to compel the unconditional submission of the Khonds, involving the surrender of their Patriarchs, and of some officers of the late Rajah, who had taken refuge with them, and a promise for the future, to yield to us the obedience and the services which had been given to Goomsur, that obedience being supposed to comprehend submission to the authority of a "Bissye" of our appointment.

14. No opposition was offered to our advance. But the Khonds refused with the most admirable constancy, to bring their natural heads, or their guests, bound to our scaffolds. The country was laid utterly desolate. The population was unceasingly pursued by the troops. At the end of about two months, the Rajah's Hindu officers were given up for a reward in the Maliahs of *Boad*. The

Patriarchs of the offending District of Goomsur were betrayed one by one through the Naieks of the border, and the Hindu inhabitants of the hills ; with the exception of the chief Dora Bissye who, favored or feared by all, escaped to the Patna Zemindary, from whence, having obtained the promise of his life from the Commissioner for Cuttack, he sometime after came in.

15. The Khond Chiefs of Baramootah were condemned and executed almost without exception.

16. Sunnuds, of the exact terms of which I am not informed, were given generally to their supposed heirs.

17. Sam Bissye, the *Hindu* employe of the Khonds of Hodzoghoro, a District recently connected with *Boad*, was invested with the authority supposed to belong to the office of the chief Bissye of the Rajah of Goomsur, aud with a title, in the room of the federal Khond Patriarch Dora Bissye.

18. By Act XXIV. of 1839 the Zemindaries of the Ganjam and Vizagapatam Districts, with the territories of the connected Tribes, were removed from the operation of the rules for the administration of Civil and Criminal Justice and for the collection of Revenue, and placed under Agents instructed by the Government of Fort St. George.

19. These Agents administer the established Criminal law under slightly modified rules of procedure. They administer the Civil law and the Revenue law modified in like manner, with these principal exceptions that questions of disputed succession to Zemindary Estates, and to lands held on any species of tenure analogous to the feudal, are not determined judicially, but decided by the Government upon the report of the Agent, as questions of policy, and in cases in which landed property, held on these tenures, and of considerable value, is involved, an appeal lies from the decision of the Agent, not to the Court of Sudr Adawlut, but to the Governor in Council.

20. Our authority is acknowledged, in any degree, in the Khond Districts of Goomsur alone, which our arms reduced. And no permanent advantage has attended the efforts which have been made towards the abolition of the rite of human sacrifices.

21. Thus it appears, that we first met the mountain Khonds of Goomsur as the ancient and religiously pledged allies, and at the same time the hosts of its rebel Zemindar, with whom from their situation, and from our policy, they had necessarily exclusive relations. A portion of them, in profound ignorance of the character, and the objects of our power, blindly offered resistance, and suffered the extreme penalties of rebellion.

22. We have heretofore necessarily met the Hill Tribes of Orissa every where else in the same character alone, viz. as allies of Zemindars in revolt. Thus did we first encounter the Khonds North of the Mahanuddee, arrayed on the side

of the rebel Rajah of Khoordah and under circumstances nearly analogous as I am informed, occurred our first collision with the Koles, over whom we have since established a direct influence, and thus did we meet the still undescribed Sourah race leagued more or less permanently with the rebel Chiefs of Vizianagram, Golcondah, Kimedy and Palcondah.

23. And for the future, there exists the same risk of collision with other sections of the hill population, as the allies of numerous Chiefs of extensive and little known Domains in the Districts of Ganjam and Vizagapatam, besides the risk which may arise from our being in immediate contact with them.

24. Now, our leading objects with respect to these Tribes are, I conceive, necessarily these—1st, as a matter of policy to induce their acknowledgment of our supremacy, and to establish relations with them as subjects which shall supersede their exclusive relations with the Zemindaries as allies—2dly, with reference to their religion ; to effect the abolition of the rite of human sacrifices, and it is plain that the first condition of the accomplishment of these objects is peace.

25. The risk of future collision with them as allies of the Zemindars, may, I apprehend, from the history of the past, be obviated in a great degree by measures addressed to the latter. The consideration of those measures does not fall within the scope of this paper. But it may be observed in passing, with reference to our power to repeat such contests as that which occurred in Goomsur, that the force which was assembled there in the second year, amounted to nearly one half of the Madras troops of the line which, the army being then distributed at its usual stations, were available for foreign service, and that the sufferings of those troops from sickness, during the first year, was greater than has been recorded of any other force whatsoever.

26. The relation which it is proposed to establish with the Khonds as subjects, must necessarily form the foundation of any system of means through which we may attempt to effect the desired modification of their religious rites.

27. I shall consider the principles of that relation, and the mode in which it may be possible to establish it amongst this class of means, in the next Section.

SECTION II.

Of Measures to be adopted with reference to the Religion of the Khonds.

28. It is desired to effect the abolition of the rite of human sacrifice in the religious ceremonial of this race ; that rite being an act of worship which is of the very essence the vital fact of their superstition, forming in one point of view its sum ; and which, moreover, is sanctioned, by the practice of the only other religion by the authority of the only civilization which is known to them.

29. It is well established, that the moral character of the Khonds is eminently distinguished by the power to resist coercion.

30. The territory which is partially inhabited by them and by the Sourahs, both being similarly connected with Zemindars over whom our authority has never been practically established, extends over a space 300 miles in length, and from 50 to 100 in breadth, between the Mahanuddee and the Godavery ; and is included partly in the Madras, partly in the Bengal Territories, and partly within the limits of Nagpore. It is composed of forest, swamps, and mountain fastnesses interspersed with open and productive vallies ; and from its climate is habitable with safety by strangers, only during a few months in the year.

31. Thus, in a word the character of the Khonds, and the physical nature of their country combine, to preclude any attempt to effect the suppression of their great religious rite by force as a primary measure.

32. It remains to consider what other means exist, or may be created for the accomplishment of this object.

33. As to the efficacy of the measures which I shall attempt to indicate, I venture to express the strictly conditional opinion, that the prospect of success appears to me to be such as to authorize a systematic attempt to attain it. That a long, laborious, and fortunate course of exertion may ultimately achieve the desired purpose, which has rarely been surpassed in difficulty and delicacy, while I think it certain that such exertion, to whatever extent it shall proceed, will be productive of beneficial effects alone.

34. I shall trace in general terms, what seem to me to be the proper principles of procedure. It being distinctly understood that in my opinion, the information necessary to the formation of a detailed system of measures is still to be acquired.

SECTION III.

THE KHONDS, SOUTH OF THE MAHANUDDEE, SHOULD BE INCLUDED IN ONE PLAN OF OPERATIONS.

35. I may premise by stating that, in my judgment all the Khond Tribes, south of the Mahanuddee, whether in the Bengal or the Madras Territories, should be included in one plan of operations, directed by a single Agent.

36. The Tribes connected with Boad, Duspullah, and Goomsur, for example, of which the two former Zemindaries are in the Cuttack, the latter in the Ganjam District, may be said, in some sort, to belong to one social system. They are all linked together in some degree, by ties of interest or of feeling ; and any difference in their treatment would preclude all chance of their acquiring distinct ideas of the character, or confidence in the objects of our power. While experience proves, what their character would lead us to anticipate, that where concessions are to be made, they will far more readily embrace a common than a various lot. These views were strongly impressed upon my mind, upon the following occasion.

37. The Rajah of Boad was required in 1836 by the authorities on the South Western Frontier of Bengal, but in terms which are not precisely known to me, to announce to the Tribes of his Zemindary the abhorrence of the Government of the Meria rite, and to exert his authority for its suppression.

38. He represented to me, then at Boad that, as I knew it was in his power to yield even a formal obedience to this order in the case of many of the Khond Districts, only if his messengers were allowed the protection of my camp, and that protection I very willingly gave, as the occasion promised to afford me valuable opportunities of observation.

39. A considerable degree of alarm followed the receipt above the Ghauts of the communications of the Rajah, which were, I believe, made in very vague and various terms to the different Chief Patriarchs.

40. Councils met every where. The whole population was deeply agitated, and all friendly intercourse with me ceased. In the remote and sequestered District of Ruttabarri it was believed that I was come to enforce compliance with the mandates, and on arriving there, I found that active preparations had commenced for resistance. Very serious results threatened, when the opportune appearance upon the scene of the great Khonro of Boad, whose friendship I had previously made, removed every difficulty.

41. The Khonds could arrive at no distinct conclusion respecting the real meaning of the intimations which were thus made to them; and, under all the circumstances, it was exceedingly difficult for me to give any explanation of them. But the Tribes having made out that no coercive measures were then intended, and that I, at least, was there with views purely friendly, they gradually became at ease, and laid their minds bare to me on the whole subject.

42. In the end, they consented, without much difficulty, to deliver up their victim-children to me, as other Tribes have done to other officers; and not as signifying the slightest intention to relinquish the rite, but as a peace offering, or a mark of deference for our power. But to this surrender they assented, only on the express condition that the Tribes of Goomsur should also be required to give up their victims. The Meria children they looked upon merely as property of a certain value, and as victims which could be immediately replaced. Their real and deepest anxiety was, lest they should even seem to submit to a necessity which was not acknowledged by all the Tribes within their social sphere.

43. As the authorities on either side of the Mahanuddee did not on this occasion act in concert, the necessary requisition could not at the moment be effectually made in Goomsur for the fulfilment of the condition stipulated, and so the victims were not liberated; and the Tribes were left bewildered between the apparently discrepant councils of the two Governments.

44. I may remark here what I should have supposed to be self-evident, but for much proof to the contrary, that nothing can be effected, in any case, either by

the simple liberation of victims which can be replaced ; or by the prevention of sacrifices at any particular time, or in any single district, when they can be performed, at some sacrifice of convenience, elsewhere, and at another season. Had these victims in the Boad Maliahs been liberated I was afterwards distinctly informed that a larger number must have suffered in their stead.

45. I venture, then, to express with some confidence the opinion, that the same general measures, conducted by the same agency, should embrace the whole of the mountain Khond population South of the Mahanuddee, whether included in the Madras or in the Bengal Presidency.

46. Co-operation must also, without doubt, be required on the part of the Government of Nagpore.

SECTION IV.

What relation we shall establish with the Khond Tribes as subjects.

47. Amongst the measures by the combination and gradual developement of which it may be hoped to acquire direct authority over the Khonds, with a view to the accomplishment of the desired change in their religious ceremonial, I have said that I regard the assertion of our supremacy over them, and the establishment of distinct relations with them as subjects, as necessarily the first and the most important.

48. My view of the nature of this relation and of the mode in which it may be established is this.

49. It is obvious, that the voluntary and permanent acknowledgment of our sovereignty by these rude societies, must depend upon our ability to discharge beneficially and acceptably towards them, some portion of the duties of sovereignty that they will spontaneously yield allegiance to us, only in return for advantages which are suited in form, and in spirit, to their leading ideas and to their social wants.

50. Now it appears distinctly that the great social defect of these clusters of Tribes—a defect which they have in some quarters feebly attempted to remedy is, the want of a supreme controlling authority—of a power able to arbitrate betwixt different Tribes, and betwixt Tribes and the Zemindaries, and this want I think, we may by direct and by indirect menas, to a certain extent, supply—claiming and receiving allegiance in return—and laying the foundation of a general ascendancy.

51. The Patriarchal authority suffices for the maintenance of order and security within each Tribe. But without, all is discord and confusion. Betwixt Tribes, are every where seen disagreements, conflicts, feuds without end and without remedy, and the Zemindars are at once the allies, and the chief enemies of each Khond society.

52. Justice betwixt independent societies is in a word, the great want which is deeply felt by all ; and I found the expectation that these Tribes may be brought to receive it at our hands to the extent which naturally gives rise to some of the sentiments of allegiance upon the fact of the general predominance of pacific feelings and interests amongst those which are known to me upon their having in Boad, besides instituting the office of federal chief—a germ of chief Magistracy—called in a set of Hindu functionaries, one of whose chief duties is the settlement of feuds ; upon the consideration that rude men are universally prove to yield a high degree of moral obedience to civilized power when judiciously and benevolently exhibited, and finally upon this fact in my limited experience—that the heads of the few Tribes whose confidence I had an opportunity to gain, acting instinctively from the necessity of their situation uniformly desired to make me the arbiter of those differences with other Tribes, with which there existed no native authority competent to deal.

53. What we may require of these societies, on the other hand, as subjects, is, in my opinion, simply this. That a Tribe shall in no case aid any other party against us, while it shall yield us active assistance when we can engage to discharge towards it the reciprocal duty of protection—and this obligation of defence it is plain that we must, until specially prepared for it, be very cautious in undertaking, lest we incur the risk of evils greater than those which we would remove ; viz. the risk of those which attend war in the region of the Ghauts.

54. The only forms of public authority of which the Khonds have any idea are their own partriarchal form, and the tyrannies of the Zemindars. And our authority, to be accepted, must bear, unequivocally, both the external aspect and the spirit of the former, as the Tribes of North America first submitted to the Sovereigns of England only as their Great Father.

55. It is plain, that while our supremacy should be acknowledged by significant forms distinct from those by which the rank of the Zemindars has been hitherto recognized, we should carefully avoid the imposition of any onerous conditions, or marked badges of vasalage, upon a people in the last degree jealous both of the form and the substance of liberty.

56. Such, in general terms, is my idea of the nature of the relation which may be established between the Government and those Tribes as subjects, and in the first instance chiefly through our power to minister to their leading social want.

SECTION V.

Of the mode of introducing our authority amongst the Khond Tribes.

57. As to the mode of introducing the idea of allegiance to us amongst these Tribes, (whose conceptions of the rights and duties of separate societies I have already stated,) it appears to me to be plain, in the first place, that allegiance must here be understood to mean vaguely and generally a sense of deference for our power, and our civilization, combined with feelings of attachment arising from the

experience or from the expectation of the beneficial exercise of the former; and secondly, that we can approach the Khonds to communicate new ideas of this or of any other class through their patriarchal heads alone.

58. Our first object must therefore be to win those heads to our purpose, and this is to be accomplished—1st, through the personal influence of the Agent of Government—2ndly, by addressing to them individually, every form of direct and indirect inducement which their character and situation indicate as likely to prevail.

Through the personal influence of the Agent.

59. To establish personal influence, I believe that there is but one mode of procedure. The Agent must pitch his tent with each Tribe until he is regarded by its heads as their best friend, until they are fully assured of his perfect knowledge of its situation, and of his sympathy with it. The only unequivocal proof of their confidence being their distinct and fixed desire to make him the arbiter of their most important interests, with which their own institutions are too weak to deal, and as before observed, so far as my limited observations go, the tendency to invest him with this character, when the condition of personal confidence is fulfilled, is universal.

60. The first foundations of the general authority which we seek to build up are to be laid through a wise exercise of the power which may thus be conceded.

Through direct inducements.

61. As to direct inducements to subservience to our views, there fortunately exists one object of desire to the Khonds, through which, in some situations at least, the heads of society may be very powerfully swayed.

Through gifts of land.

62. Every Khond has a passionate desire to possess land; and it were fortunate if the Tribes of the Eastern face of the Ghauts could be won by the grant of all the nearly valueless jungle tracts of Goomsur and Sooradah, and if those upon the Mahanuddee could be gained by the similar wastes of Boad and Duspullah.

63. Had each chief Patriarch of the Goomsur Maliahs, for example, a home in the low country where he might occasionally reside without being permanently separated from his Tribe, he himself, his family and his dependants would acquire new ideas, new tastes, new wants; would become familiar with Hindu society and accustomed to easy intercourse with the officers of Government, would be brought immediately within the sphere of any influences which we chose to address to them, —ultimately, perhaps, direct education might be brought to bear upon them.

64. The risk to be guarded against would be, lest by conferring upon these Patriarchs separate and independent property, in a situation where they must acquire new manners, and become involved in new interests, they should become estranged from and should lose influence over their Tribes.

By gifts of money, cattle, &c.

65. Gifts of money, cattle, &c. are the remaining most obvious incentives to co-operation, or rewards of exertion, which may be presented to the Patriarchs,—and conveniently given to them in return for their yearly offerings of homage, or for those made upon their accession to office.

Through titles, &c.

66. A very considerable degree of inflnence may be exerted through dresses of honor, titles, and honorary privileges any accidental epithet; a complimentary nick-name given by "the Rajah" becomes hereditary, and is as tenaciously adhered to by a Khond family as a title of nobility is in Europe.

By employment in the public service.

67. Lastly, I regard the employment of the Khonds in public services suited to the peculiarities of their character and situation, as amongst the most important means at our disposal for the accomplishment of the objects proposed.

68. The formation of a Bheel Corps, which was gradually subjected to discipline in the Bombay Presidency, has been found to change entirely the character of the portion of that people to which the measure was applied.

An experimental Khond levy.

69. I am aware of the leading distinctions betwixt the manners of that race and those of the Khonds. But I believe that the measure of disciplining a small body of Khonds would be found in the highest degree effectual to create sentiments of attachment to our Agents, and to our power, and to lead to the establishment of our direct authority. In any event it would afford the best means of acquiring a clear insight into the character and disposition of the Khond people, and would enable us to give them many true impressions of our powers. It may become a most important means for the diffusion amongst them of the first seeds of civilization, and finally, a devoted band of Khonds would be an invaluable instrument in our future dealings with any of the other mountain races of Orissa.

70. Nor is it to be lost sight of, that, whatever species of connection may arise between us and these Tribes, it may become necessary to assert our supremacy over them by force. The occurrence of that necessity is to be most effectually prevented by their conviction that our means to make our power respected are instant and irresistible. Having in our service a body of the mountain population would necessarily add great strength to such a conviction.

SECTION VI.

Of measures more especially directed to the abolition of the rite of Human Sacrifice.

71. Such, in general terms, are the measures by which it appears to me that we may endeavour to establish a direct authority over these Tribes through our power to minister to some of their social wants, and to act upon some of the leading tendencies of their character.

72. I shall next attempt to state in like manner the means which may be combined with that general authority with an special view to the suppression of the rite of human sacrifice.

We must gain the Priesthood to our views.

73. I conceive, that with reference to this object our first endeavour must be to attain influence over the priesthood, by the systematic use of every means

which the minutest knowledge of their habits and situation may suggest, it being carefully observed that the Patriarchs are always to be regarded as virtually, if not professionally, priests. The mode of gaining the priesthood of the portion of the country which may be selected as most favorable for the commencement of any system of operations, must be expressly studied as a subject of the first moment, and of the greatest difficulty, its mastery being plainly essential to any degree of success.

74. As a subordinate object, we must also obtain the cordial co-operation of the Zemindars connected with the Khond population. Their direct influence is generally great with some tribe or section, and they alone can afford the minute local information respecting persons and things which is necessary to formation of any plan of operations. They may themselves be powerfully acted upon by honorary gifts and privileges, or by the prospect of a remission of Tribute in the event of success. They would all, so far as I know, be well pleased to see the Khonds acknowledge our authority.

Obtain the co-operation of the Zemindars.

75. While for the reasons above stated we are precluded from the use of force as a primary measure it is to be carefully kept sight of as a secondary means. If we shall gain the mass, the great majority of any Tribe, it may be highly advantageous, and quite possible to coerce individuals.

Employ force as a secondary measure.

76. The fittest instrument of such coercion, when its propriety shall unequivocally appear, is matter of important consideration.

77. The Naicks and Peons who hold lands of Goomsur and the other Zemindaries on the condition of keeping the borders, are by their local knowledge and their power of bearing the climate, best adopted to such service; but they have this disqualification, that they are generally inspired by the strongest feelings of antipathy towards the Khonds.

78. Our company of Sebundies at Ganjam is a better instrument for this purpose. A small levy of Khonds who had relinquished the Meria rite, and who had been brought to transfer to an officer some portion of their devotedness to a Patriarchal leader, were, as observed above, an instrument in every point of view beyond price. My hope that such a force may be created, however, rests in some degree upon the impressions of others respecting the population of Districts which I have not visited.

SECTION VII.

Of legal provisions for the punishment of the offence of traffic in human victims.

79. With reference to the important subject of the legal punishment of persons engaged in the sale and purchase of human victims, the following considerations present themselves.

80. There appear to be five distinct classes of persons engaged in this traffic either as sellers, or as purchasers, or in both characters.

1st. There are the Mountain Khonds. In them the purchase is not a moral offence, and against them it is at present generally impossible to enforce any law.

2ndly. There are the families of the Panwa and other Hindu castes, hereditarily resident on the Hills, whose express office is the provision of victims. They are socially as above stated* completely identified with the Khonds, and are esteemed most important members of every community. While, therefore, our information does not suffice to determine exactly their moral situation, there would be as much difficutly in enforcing the law against them as against the Khonds by whom they are protected.

* Part V. Para. 17.

3rdly. There is a class of procurers by buying and by kidnapping, generally of the above mentioned, and the other Pariah castes of Orissa, whose home is the low country.

4thly. The Khonds of the low country are, as I am informed, occasionally engaged in procuring victims to be carried up the hills for sale and sacrifice ; they themselves participating in the rite, while they bear a share of the expense. The procuring the victims is with these Khonds an act of religion, but the law could be partially enforced against them.

5thly. There are the Hindus who sell the victims to the procurers. They are generally persons in the last stage of destitution, very frequently widows, who thus dispose of their own children or of children of whom they have charge ; but probably in many or most cases without knowing the purpose for which they are purchased.

81. Now these distinctions, in so far as they depend upon differences in local and moral situation which do not admit of exact definition, cannot plainly be recognized by the law, with reference to either race. The same penalties must attach to the offence, wherever, and by whomsoever committed ; discretionary power as to their application being confided to the Judge.

82. But the Agent to Government can alone determine against whom it is possible, or expedient with a view to the accomplishment of the objects proposed, to execute the law. He must, in a word, have the anomalous power to enforce or to suspend the operation of the law, at least with respect to two classes of the population, viz., to all Khonds, and to the Panwa and other procurers who reside amongst and are identified with the Hill Khonds.

83. That it should be necessary, to make it discretional with an Agent to afford or deny justice where we affect jurisdiction, is no doubt, a great evil. But to withhold such discretion here to leave it even in semblance *imperative* in any case, upon the Agent to attempt to establish the jurisdiction of his own or of any other Court, were to risk the entire defeat of the objects proposed.

84. In the only case of prosecution on record for the abduction and sale of a victim to the Khonds, the case of Yenady Bemoe, a procurer tried at Chicacole at the 2nd Sessions of 1837, the necessity for the exercise of this discretion was admitted. The prisoner having been acquitted of a first charge upon technical grounds, was ordered by the Superior Court to be tried on a second charge of which he was plainly guilty. But proceedings were necessarily abandoned, upon the Magistrate's (now the Agent to the Governor in Ganjam) declaring that it was highly inexpedient to attempt to enforce in the hill Districts the preliminary processes of the Court.

85. Against the Hindu procurers of the low country, and against the Hindu sellers of children as victims, there can, I presume, be no question that most rigorous laws should be enforced, and if necessary, by a special Agency, as in the case of Thuggee.

86. The Madras Regulations provide no punishment for the crime of traffic in human victims. By the Mahomedan law it is punishable at the discretion of the Court ; and no one having yet *been convicted of the offence no penalty for it has been declared.

* July 1841.

87. Procurers should, in my judgment, be invariably punished by transportation for life: a penalty which I believe to be in general as much dreaded in Orissa as death.

88. It will be exceedingly difficult to prove against the sellers of children, the knowledge of the object of the purchasers, which is essential to render them criminal in the same degree.

89. But the magnitude of the evil to society with which we are attempting to contend, with such inadequate means, obviously sanctions, without reference to the degree of moral guilt of the offender, our constituting the sale of children on *any pretence whatever* an offence to be repressed by the severest penalties.

90. I therefore venture to suggest, that in the Districts from which victims are drawn, the penalty of transportation for life should be attached to this offence: a large discretion being left to the Judge, and at them all feuds are forgotten.

91. I would suggest that the Agent to the Governor should be authorized to delegate the power of trying this offence to an Assistant, which, if the punishment proposed shall be adopted, his present instructions do not permit.

92. It appears to me to be of so much consequence that judicial proceedings with respect to this offence should be summary, and that they should be conducted exclusively on the responsibility of the local agency, that I would suggest that sentences passed by the Agent should be carried into execution without confirmation by the Foujdaree Adawlut.

SECTION VIII.

Of Roads and Fairs in the Khond Country.

93. Important and immediate effects have been expected by some, from the promotion of intercourse between the Khonds and the surrounding Hindu population by opening roads through the region of the Ghauts, and by the establishment of fairs.

94. With respect to the efficacy of the former measure as a means of civilization, we can appeal to clear experience. A road which, except at a few points, is by nature nearly level, runs through the Khond Districts of Chokapaud, Nowsagur, and Atcombo, from Goomsur to Boad by it, Brinjarry camps and travellers of all descriptions have passed in general numbers from the remotest times, the former generally carrying grain and iron from the Districts of Choteesgur and Sumbhulpore, to be exchanged upon the coast for salt and cloth.

95. In a few of the principal villages on this route, and occupying a distinct quarter in each, a small number of Hindu families are settled, either as cultivators, as dependents of the Hindu Bissyes, or as traders ; and the following are the effects which seem to have arisen from the ancient intercourse of the two races.

96. The Khonds build their villages (as they do on the plateau in this quarter) in the Hindu form, generally, and understand the Ooriah language, though imperfectly, and wear the single piece of cloth which constitutes their dress something in the Hindu fashion. The Patriarchs all affect Hindu manners in a greater or less degree. They generally learn from the Brahmins to read and write, and are familiar with the legends of the Puranas which are here most popular. They generally gave me to understand, in hinting their claims to advancement beyond their brethren of the recesses of the Ghauts, that they believed in the Hindu Gods—but without any disparagement to their own divinities: And it appeared to me that the Hindus generally returned the philosophical compliment.

97. I could discover in the Khonds on this route, no evidence of any tendency towards the relinquishment of the opinion—not of the efficacy but of the indispensable necessity of human sacrifices ; towards any change in their religious ideas, save what may be implied in the partial introduction of Hindu priests for the worship of Kali, and some local gods, and the combination, or confusion of the worship of Kali with that of the Earth God.

98. The Brinjarries in their camps offer human victims to Kali, and generally, it is said, at the beginning and at the completion of each undertaking.

99. Three easy Ghauts for loaded cattle (two of which were made by the Sappers) already connect Goomsur with the great plateau. As there is an abundant supply of water amongst the hills in the months when the route by Chokapaud is nearly impassable from drought, to cattle even in small numbers, the Brinjarries,

many of whom came to talk to me upon the subject, expressed anxiety for the establishment of a route over the plateau direct from Sohnpore, avoiding Boad, if they could be assured of protection, and of freedom from heavier imposts than those which they now pay, at Boad to the Rajah; at Raneegunze to the Khonro; at Bonee to the Patriarch of Nowsagur; and at Gottegooda to the Khonds of Chokapaud; in short on the frontiers of each Zemindary and Khond District.

100. The active application of civilizing influences can alone, I believe, remove barbarism. But in our dearth of means, we can afford to omit no attempt even to increase the intercourse of the Khonds with the scarcely less rude Hindus by whom they are surrounded.

101. The first effect, however, which would arise from opening a new and a preferable route across the Ghauts from Goomsur to Sohnpore, would be to transfer the customs levied on the transit of goods from one set of tribes to another set, producing a feeling of injury in the former whom the change would impoverish; while, it may be added, it would probably render the Boad Rajah unable to pay his tribute. The settlement of the tolls to be levied on the new line would, I apprehend, be matter of great difficulty. I do not know enough of the direction or tendencies of commerce in other portions of the Ghauts, or of the practicability of forming routes over them, to speak with confidence of the probable effects of opening roads elsewhere.

102. Fairs, which shall be found to tend to draw these tribes from their fastnesses into friendly and familiar contact with other men, and to enlarge the circle of their wants, are very plainly advantageous, and should be carefully multiplied. I may however observe that I have heard the low state of civilization of the population of some of the Goomsur Maliahs, compared with those of Boad; ascribed with much show of reason to the circumstance, that, from the existence of fairs which have been established in the former quarter at the bases of the Ghauts, no Hindu merchants reside habitually in them.

SECTION IX.

Of the Agency required for the execution of these measures.

103. It appears to me obvious, that we may attempt by means of a special agency alone, European and Native, to accomplish the work which is here proposed.

104. Its very nature, I conceive, plainly precludes its accomplishment departmentally by any one: requires that it shall be committed, virtually at least, as a separate labour, to an Agent free from minute responsibility, empowered to realize according to his own views, measures of which the Government shall indicate the principles.

105. All arrangements, all agreements which can now be made with the Khond Tribes, will be, virtually, personal compacts between the Patriarchs and the

officer who makes them, and, to be understood, they must be final, not conditional, upon the approval of their details by another mind which necessarily contemplates them from a different point of view. A single case of reversal would almost inevitably overthrow any fabric of confidence which skill might raise. We cannot, it appears to me, with any hope of success practically exhibit to this people or to any people in their situation, our authority under a graduated form.

106. Farther, provision must plainly be made to maintain the uninterrupted application of any system of measures which may be adopted towards these Tribes, to keep up the traditional knowledge of persons and events which is necessary to the adoption of any system to ever changing circumstances.

107. A subordinate Native Agency must also be carefully formed. Hindus are every where seen settled in small numbers throughout the hill country, in the service of the Zemindars, or of the Tribes, or as merchants. We must instruct the ablest of this class in our views, and it will probably be found convenient to fix the attention of a Native Agent upon each Tribe, or cluster, as is the custom of the Zemindars, when they desire to sway particular sections of the Khonds. The Soodoo caste in Boad, which has from time immemorial been peculiarly connected with the Khond population, will supply us with able instruments in that quarter.

108. The difficulty of procuring persons fit to be the medium of confidential intercourse between us and the Khonds is very great. I selected to aid me in obtaining information above the Ghauts, four persons considered the most competent in the Ganjam District. All were willing and intelligent men, acting under the hope of reward, but they were of no manner of use. They could not acquire in the necessary degree the confidence of a single Khond Chief. But for the extraordinary tact and intelligence of Bawah Khan, a Mussulman, in my own employment, I should scarcely have been able to learn in that country a single fact relative to the Khond people, with a degree of accuracy which would have justified me in recording it.

109. There appear to me to be strong grounds to hope that it may be possible to employ the invaluable agency of the Khond Patriarch of Goomsur, Dora Bissye.

(Signed) S. C. MACPHERSON, *Lieut.*,
Assistant Agent to the Governor of Fort St. George, in Ganjam.

MADRAS,
14*th September*, 1841.

(A true copy,)

HENRY CHAMIER,
Chief Secretary.

APPENDIX.

NOTE I.

(Vide P. 14, Para. 21.)

Analysis of Population in the Town of Boad, including all the Castes in the Zemindary.

No.	Caste	*Houses.*
1.	Oriya Brahmins—Jarwa Brahmins,	40
2.	Santo Bypool, illegitimate children of Boad Rajah, ditto,	12
3.	Military and other honorable service living on Enam land,	
4.	Mhanti Curnums in Rajah's service—have Enam land,	10
5.	Bhoolia Weavers, (exclusively of white cloth,)	50
6.	Koolia Weavers, (of red thread, coarse silk, &c.,)	15
7.	Soodoo Peons and Agriculturists,	10
	Doomalo Gonro bring water for Rajah and Brahmin, sell milk and act as peons,	10
8.	Dooma in Oriya means hollow thing hung round bullocks' necks, —Herd Cows,	
9.	Moghodo Gonro, something less in caste than these,	4
10.	Apoto Gonro bring water to Rajah,	2
11.	Drooliya Gonro bullock herdsmen,	1
12.	Boondary or Barbers,	5
13.	Dhoba,	5
14.	Koomaro, Potters,	3
15.	Kent, River Fishermen,	20
16.	Gingria, fishers of shrimps, &c. with pole net,	3
17.	Kossari, Brass Smiths,	2
18.	Kodra, or Copper Smiths,	3
19.	Teli, Oilmen,	3
20.	Boomia, Goldsmiths,	5
21.	Gooriya, Sugar and Confectioner,	2
22.	Panwa, beyond fort not Hindus. Coarse Cloth Weavers,	10
23.	Kuddi, Sweepers lower than Panwa,	10
24.	Rona, Gardeners,	10
25.	Mali, growers of flowers for worship and poojaries,	2
26.	Moochi, Shoemaker,	1
27.	Koira, Peons and Cultivators,	2
28.	Oriya, Peons and Cultivators,	2
29.	Musselmen,	4
30.	Panwa,	2
31.	Byragi, settled,	1
32.	Soondi, sell Liquors,	4
33.	Khond, a Peon,	1

34.	Boghodo, Khond,	1
35.	Pundit, Physician and Astrologer,	2
36.	Rajpoot Peons,	3
37.	Lanri, Shave, Paria Castes,	2
38.	Gondo, Gonds,	3
39.	Bavan, Carpenter,	2
40.	Saur, Peons,	2
41.	Moolia, Coolies,	1
	Total,......	270

NOTE II.

(P. 15, Para. 22.)

Chief vegetable products of the Zemindaries of Goomsur and Boad and of their connected Khond Districts above and below the Ghauts.

The following are the most important vegetable products of the region included in the Map. The names first given are Orissan. Their Hindoostanee synonymes are marked H. Those cultivated on the table land above the Ghauts have T prefixed.

Rice, 18 Sorts.	
Grains,—Mundia or (H) Raggi.	Elensine Stricta.
(T) Kundaloo or (H) Tuar.	Cytisus Cajan.
(H) Cooltee.	Dolichos Biflorus.
Beeree or (H) Mash.	Phascolus radiatus.
(T) Kangoo (H) Makka or Indian Corn.	
(T) (H) Sursoo or Mustard.	Sinapis Dichotoma.
(T) Joorunga or (H) Lobe, a bean.	
Mooggo or (H) Moonga.	Phaseolus Mungo.
Oils—(T) Kulso or (H) Erindi.	Ricinus Communis.
Russi or (H) Til.	Sesamum Orientale.
(T H) Ram Til.	Verbesina Sativa.
(H) Kurring.	
Vegetables,—(T) Sumbae or (H) Sumbi.	
(T) Jotta or (H) Sem.	Dolichos.
Saroo or (H) Kuchoo or Yam.	Arum.
Mossia or (H) Doola Kunda, a similar root.	
Kondomoollo.	Arum.
(T) Kowria Saggo Ambari ki Bajee.	
(T) Byugan Brinjal.	Solamun Melongena.
Pyaz, Onion.	Allium Cefa.
Russina (H) Russun, Garlick.	Allium Sativum.
(T) Boctaloo (H) Shukhur Kuddo, pumpkin.	Curcurbita.

(T) Rukkaroo (H) Hurya Kuddo, green do.	Curcurbita.
(T) Jonni (H) Toorei, of Cucumber kind.	
(T) Potlakaia (H) Chilchunda do.	
Kakoori (H) Kumkeeri, Melon.	
Bhendi.	
(T) Lonka Mircho.	Capsicum Annumu.
(H) Karela.	Cleome Pentapylla.
Jungle Fruits (T) Kakoora.	Curcuma.
(T) Kendo.	
(T) Koito and (H) Kuweet.	
(T) Mossia.	
(T) Korwa, in Telloogoo Pilleeyello kunda.	
(T) Konkora.	Cucumis.
(T) Bello (H) Bell.	
Other plants of economical value.	
Coppa.	Gossypium Herbaceum Cotton.
Dhooan Tobacco.	
Panno, Betel only in the Brahmin villages.	Peper Betel.
Akkoo, Sugar Cane.	
Jennup (H) Sunn.	Crotolarea Juncea.
Fruits,—(T) Ambo, Mango.	Mangefern Sudica.
(T) Ponso, Jack fruit.	
(T) Kojala, Plantain.	Musa Paradisiaca.
Noodia, Cocoa-nut, rarely seen.	Cocos Nucifera.
Jaunnie, Guava.	
Limbo, Lime.	Citrus Acida.
(T) Tobba.	
Salo, Palmira.	Torassia Hobulliformis.
Dalimo, Pomegranate.	Punica Granatum.

NOTE III.

(P. 16, Para. 26.)

Hindoo Castes of the North Eastern Districts of Goomsur.

1.	Buddri, Brahmins.	In charge of the Temples.
2.	Dunwa, Brahmins.	Astrologers, Officiate at Marriages and other feasts, live only in Agrarums.
3.	Tuswa or Holwa, ditto.	Farmers, and eat flesh, reside in common villages.
4.	Soondi	Distil Arrack, make Sugar, and act as Peons.
5.	Koormoo	Prevail in these Mootahs, Cultivator and Peons.

6. Oriyah.................................. Agriculturists and Peons.
7. Dulwa.................................. Prevail about Goomsur and Behrampore and are ditto ditto.
8. Soobya Gonra....................... Cow feeders and farmers.
9. Kolta Gonra. .... Ditto ditto.
10. Moghoda ditto, ... Ditto ditto, and Peons.
11. Bowdya. .... Farmers and Peons, generally diffused.
12. Sugwa or Pondra. .... Gardeners.
13. Kalinjee. .... Farmers and Peons, high caste.
14. Koomaroo. .... Potters and Farmers, never Peons.
15. Coira. .... Farmers and Peons.
16. Doba. .... Washermen, Farmers and Peons.
17. Bundary.
18. Gooriya. .... Sugar makers, Peons and Merchants.
19. Bonnea. .... Peons, &c.
20. Panwa. .... Cloth makers, never Peons.
21. Mhanti or Corono or Kayet. ... Curnums, &c.
22. Komti. .... Merchants,
23. Toangla. .... Sugar makers and Peons.
24. Soura. .... Farmers and Peons.
25. Gainta................................ Ditto Ditto.
26. Malodumbo.
27. Tely.................................... Oil sellers and Merchants.
28. Rungrez. .... Colormen.

Not Hindoos.

29. Chichori or Huddee. .... Sweepers, Umbrella makers, beat Tomtoms.
30. Kodalo or Bowry. .... Bearers.
31. Dumbo. .... Basket and Mat-makers.

NOTE IV.

(Page 16—Para. 25.)

The Geological features of a part of Goomsur and of Boad.

The great Gneiss deposit of this portion of India appears exclusively as the fundamental rock of these tracts.

It's structure, constitution, and external aspects are infinitely diversified. It's prevailing forms and superficial features are these—

Throughout extensive tracts, it is a hard Granitic rock of close granular texture, composed of smoky Quartz, with minute crystals of dull red Felspar, and occasional scales of mica, obscurely stratified, and wasting in low flat domes.

In other districts, the character of the rock is highly crystalline. Felspar is greatly increased, proportion appears in large sized prisms, Hornblende is occasionally present. The strata affect the bedded form, and disintegrate in prismatic and cuboidol masses, picturesquely piled.

The Gneiss less frequently receives, in some tracts comparatively limited, a new character from the addition of Garnets in great quantity. By these it is pervaded, now as a close granular Quartzose rock, the Garnet sparks running in the lines of stratification, now as a finely laminar mass, the strata of which are endlessly bent and contorted. In the rock, under this form, every variety of structure, of texture, and of constitution prevails by turns. Hornstone, Felspar, Mica, Hornblende, and dark Garnets appear mingled in every proportion, and individually developed in great beauty.

The rock thus constituted generally decomposed by exfoliation in low undulating surfaces.

The Gneiss, finally, assumes throughout extensive districts as at Boad, a strongly marked porphyritic character, it's dark gray surface being strikingly variegated by prisms of Felspar from two to six inches in length, which become white on exposure.

This rock is every where traversed by Quartz veins, both transversely and in the direction of the lamina.

It is in some tracts also largely penetrated by Granitic veins on every scale, in other districts these are entirely wanting.

There occur likewise throughout this deposit occasional dykes of Greenstone or of Hornblende rock, whose course the nature of the surface renders it extremely difficult to trace. The bearing of the observed beds was nearly N. N. E.

The general direction of the Gneiss strata is N. Easterly. They are inclined at every possible angle.

At an average height of from 300 to 500 feet above the general level of the country, whether below the Ghauts, or on the plateau, the Gneiss appears to pass by gradations into sandstone, or is suddenly replaced by that rock.

This Sandstone is generally constituted of Quartz and Felspar, with mica in small quantity, interposed in the lines of stratification.

In texture it is both close and granular and open and crystalline, and of every degree of induration. In colour it is generally light gray, or of a yellowish or reddish white.

It's strata appear of every dimension, and in the low country conformable to the Gneiss. Their dip in these tracts is in some degree regular, ranging generally between 60 and 80 above the Ghauts, they are inclined at every possible angle, and towards every point of the compass.

The outline of the conical and pyramidal hills, and hog backed ridges, which result from the association of these rocks, is generally broken with slight asperities rarely continuously rugged. The naked rock is seldom exposed, save in the sharpest summits of the hills, in occasional bald domes, and in the water courses.

The difference between the angles of superficial inclination assumed by these rocks is disintegration is sufficiently striking.

The lower portion of a hill formed of Gneiss, rises at an angle between 15 and 25, its upper portion, composed of sandstone, is inclined at about 40.

The soil produced by these rocks necessarily bears every variety of character. It is in many tracts light and sandy, but from the proportion of Felspar contained in both formations and the large admixture of vegetable matter it is often also rich and loamy.

The gradual transitions of this sandstone into Gneiss, its conformability to this rock, and the entire absence of conglomerates in these tracts, tend to rank it among the primary rocks, while on the other hand the existence of a tract of sandstone apparently secondary over the granitic Gneiss at the eastern extremity of the valley near Ganjam, the character of the rocks of Cuttack, and the apparent connection of this deposit with that containing argillaceous ironstone beyond the Mahanuddee, would assign it a place as an old red sandstone. I did not observe the passage of veins from either side.

NOTE V.

Minor Subdivisions of the Khonds.

The divisions of the Khonds are distinguished by these epithets—

1. Maliah, }
2. Benniah, } Already explained.
3. Bhettiah, }
4. Moghoda.

5. Bhogero. These are Khonds who living in the low country remain of pure race, but adopt Hindoo customs, except in respect of ceasing to drink spirits and to eat fowls. Boghero is the Orissan name for a spot cleared in the jungle on a hill side.

6. Pulla Maliah. These Khonds inhabit Nowsagur, part of Duspullah, Kunnapoor and Autghur Pulla, means carrier, and the Pulla Maliah Khonds are Bearers and Peons to the Rajah.

7. Boosoontiah Khonds are similarly occupied.
8. Desee, a term for low country Khonds in the Patna Zemindary.
9. Tinki, the appellation of the Khonds who live in the advanced hill groups to the Eastward as in the Moherry hills.

10. Tongala.
11. Ganna.

STATISTICAL DETAILS.

KHALISAH OF BOAD.

Rajah Chundra Sikur Bunje Deo.

	Mootahs.	*Chiefs.*	*Places of Residence.*
1.	Koossumghur, including Kotrikia.	Hurree Krustnoo Gorotea.	
2.	Harbunga.	Gungadhur Gorotea.	Wotholosora.
3.	Ramghur.	Poorondhora Naul Gorotea.	
4.	Koradyghur.	Konto Gorotea.	Koradyghur.
5.	Machuchund.	Pormabecuda Naick.	Bogheerpilly.
6.	Moodjchund.		
7.	Byra Des with Soatmullick.	Sahrno Pudhaw Gorotea.	Teliseer.
8.	Fort of Poorna Cuttuck and Villages.	Takoora Gorotea.	
9.	The Fort of Booerah and Villages.	Mootoo Gorotea.	

Koossumghur.

Mootah, ... 225 188 77

	Villages.	*Houses.*	*Peons.*	*Ryots.*	*Chiefs.*
1.	Suthegodo, ruined.				
2.	Huthegoda, ditto.				
3.	Nowpurra, ditto.				
4.	Kotrikia,....................	20	20	10	Puttia Mullicko.
5.	Tolagaun, ...	15	20	5	Ditto.
6.	Bairasye, ...	30	40	10	Ditto.
7.	Gootzabarry, ...	20	10	10	Ditto.
8.	Karundygoodzoo, ...	30	30	0	Ditto.
9.	Gooindhapoorun, ...	10	5	5	Ditto.
10.	Oodgeeje, ...	30	20	10	Prathapo Mullicko.
11.	Gondisoro, ...	20	16	4	Sooclo Khonro.
12.	Mahalickapurra, ...	10	2	8	Sooclo Khonro.
13.	Kontiswaw, ...	30	20	10	Boli Mullicko Lutchwana Mahaliedo.
14.	Kookooty, ...	10	5	5	Ditto ditto.
15.	Baramoondah, ruined.				
16.	Boordah, ditto.				
17.	Jahbeer, ditto.				
18.	Raneesye, ditto.				
19.	Boroodee, ditto.				

	Villages.	*Houses.*	*Peons.*	*Ryots.*	*Chiefs.*
20.	Kootribarry, ...	12	6	6	Pudmanappo Mullick and Gungadhur Khon.
21.	Chinna, ditto, ...	5	3	2	Ditto.
22.	Ingalo, ...	17	7	10	Ditto.
23.	Goorisye, ...	5	3	2	Ditto.
24.	Padmathola or Podentilla,	6	4	2	Ditto.

Harbungah.

	Houses	Peons	Ryots
Mootah, ...	177	74	103

	Villages.	*Houses.*	*Peons.*	*Ryots.*	*Chiefs.*
1.	Wotholosora, ...	10	5	5	Gungadhur Gorotia.
2.	Koomary, ...	5	1	4	Ditto.
3.	Deemeria, ...	12	5	7	Ditto.
4.	Kolundah, ...	5	2	3	Ditto.
5.	Therada, ruined.				
6.	Koosasingho, ditto.				
7.	Korasingho, ditto.				
8.	Boocoosinghado, ditto.				
9.	Arracoopudthra,........ ...	20	18	2	Ditto.
10.	Dhiagato, ruined.				
11.	Soorundy, ditto.				
12.	Ranthoopurrado.				
13.	Bajegoodah, ...	30	15	15	
14.	Pahnegoro,.................	20	4	16	
15.	Telisye, ...	10	3	7	Ditto.
16.	Molicapadah, ...	15	1	14	Ditto.
17.	Semkcorodah,.....	20	10	10	Ditto.
18.	Sunkill	30	10	20	Ditto.

Ramghur.

	Houses	Peons	Ryots
Mootah, ...	114	28	90

	Villages.	*Houses.*	*Peons.*	*Ryots.*	*Chiefs.*
1.	Woragoda Cusbah,.........	4	4	4	Poorondhoro Naicks Gorotea.
2.	Thenthoolipaddy, ...	5	3	2	Ditto.
3.	Borolankole, ...	20	10	10	Lodoo Dehri.
4.	Suckooshe, ...	16	6	10	Bramha Gorotea.
5.	Dulpore, ...	15	5	10	Loteanatadhantha.
6.	Wamalo, ...	12	0	12	Dhonia Bhookta.
7.	Kunkla, ...	11	0	11	Bhiswanatha Pradhano.
8.	Purgulpore, ...	5	0	5	Dhomana Khonro.
9.	Sankootch, ...	4	0	4	Podhona Bookta.
10.	Buttgaum, ruined,				
11.	Moebar, Village of Ranee Ag^{m}.	10	0	10	Bramha Poorohit — Dhowara Bedha 10 Rs. to Boad Rajah.

Villages.	Houses.	Peons.	Ryots.	Chiefs.
12. Tellamaneery ditto, ...	12	0	12	Nobbrim Poorohit, do. 12 Rs.
13. Thuckoody, ruined.				
14. Othashe, ditto.				

Koradyghur.			
Mootah, ...	40	10	30

Villages.	Houses.	Peons.	Ryots.	Chiefs
1. Koradyghur Cusbah,......	40	10	30	Kanto Gorotea Dhowra Bedha 30 Rs.
2. Loheragurria, ruined.				
3. Muhlboori, ditto.				
4. Hautgaum, ditto.				
5. Daeeregoda, ditto,				
6. Sampooch.				
7. Kilahutta.				
8. Goondelia.				
9. Ponkal.				
10. Kiacotta.				
11. Kodjeripurra.				

Machuchund.	Houses.	Peons.	Ryots.
Mootah, ...	393	182	482

Villages.	Houses.	Peons.	Ryots.	Chiefs.
1. Konchathokondo, ruined.				
2. Boghurpully, ...	20	0	20	Porma Munda Naicko Dhanara Bedha 20 Rs.
3. Oothaneshe, ...	10	0	10	Pudmanabo Naicko do. 10 Rs.
4. Puckalkie, ...	5	0	5	Ditto Ditto, 5 Rs.
5. San Bunkra, ...	10	0	10	Seetharama Razoo.
6. Goointhapooroo, ...	5	0	5	Govinda Maprovoo.
7. Dhalaswero Ag^{m}., ...	10	0	10	Sristhara Poorohit.
8. Bhagabaro, ditto, ...	18	0	18	Lutchwana ditto.
9. Roctahury ditto,........ ...	5	0	5	Parry Panigrahi.
10. Sarsora, ...	100	0	100	Boad Rajah Dhowara Bedha, 100 Rs.
11. Bamda, ...	5	0	5	Dhoorga.
12. Kinputta, ruined.				
13. Naickpodah, ditto.				
14. Bagdoor, Ag^{m}., ...	3	0	3	Goda Sotaposta.
15. Delagoor Gondo, ruined.				
16. Dhagadoo, ruined.				
17. Lahardy Bondho, ...	10	0	10	Bahlinko Gauro Dhowara Bedha 10 Rs.
18. Narainpoor, ...	10	0	10	Ditto ditto.

Villages.	Houses.	Peons.	Ryots.	Chiefs.
19. Sidpoor, ...	5	1	4	Bahlinko Gauro Dhowara. Bedha 4 Rs.
20. Goodrabinni, ruined.				
21. Bondasothro, ...	6	0	6	Ganga Bookla ditto, 6 Rs.
22. Gonipurra, ruined.				
23. Bassundbuhal, ditto.				
24. Sonsurriakotta, ditto.				
25. Joogiberri Ag^{m}., ...	10	0	10	Khansama Suttia Nunda Poorohit.
26. Palaro, ...	5	0	5	Ditto ditto.
27. Mawoodgsingah Ag^{m}. ...	15	0	15	Pothbonapo Swasini.
28. Mariakootho, ...	11	11	11	Bugwan Mahji.
29. Thentholisingha, ...	20	20	20	Shamasoondar Rae Baboo.
30. Tootoorisingha, ...	5	0	5	Kanti Chunder Rae Sirdar.
31. Dundoopadah, ...	10	0	10	Beweertaput.
32. Kontearanee, ...	10	0	10	Sreekoranooput Naicko.
33. Dharnee, ruined.				
34. Sanamgooba, ...	20	0	20	Koorti Varsar Rae.
35. Bodoingoobah, ...	5	0	5	Byra Moothi.
36. Lombokahnee, ...	30	30	30	Seetharama Razoo Sirdar.
37. Girisingia, ...	40	40	40	Lobono Naick.
38. Loodharee Chinnee,......	50	50	50	Seetharama Razoo.
39. Moosoondi, ...	10	10	10	Dhanio Bookla.
40. Gomaripudder, ...	20	20	20	Jeetha Naicko.
41. Bulasingee, ruined.				
42. Wolinah, ditto.				
43. Zombili, ditto.				
44. Bulliapudro, ditto.				
45. Bwekapurra.				
46. Rytan of Dangawm.				
47. Lutchimpoor.				
48. Burhinghur.				
49. Lumbean.				
50. Bundriputter.				
51. Pyean,				
52. Udnia.				
53. Sanongiva.				
54. Boondaberim.				
55. Sorindi.				

Moodjcund.			
Mootah, ...	190	105	175

Villages.	Houses.	Peons.	Ryots.	Chiefs.
1. Murjadpoor ruined.				
2. Landgur, ditto.				

Villages.	Houses.	Peons.	Ryots.	Chiefs.
3. Chindighur, ditto.				
4. Surdapoor Ag^{m}., ...	10	0	10	Poorshwntuma Pundah.
5. Baleedholee, ...	20	5	15	Seriputta Sautho.
6. Koontbun, ...	10	0	10	Jajurnaut Sawmy.
7. Gooriyall, ruined.				
8. Koilaspoor, Ag^{m}., ...	10	0	10	Dheena Bandho Poorohit.
9. Jagunnautpoor.				
10. Jogothegodo, ...	20	20	20	Jogothi Mullicko Dhawan Bedha 20.
11. Kodiatholo, ...	40	10	30	Mahdhavee Ranee Dhowara Bedha 30 Rupees.
12. Maijaghur Ag^{m}., ...	10	0	10	Sathamundha Poorohit.
13. Junnapauk, ...	20	20	20	Secrabehra Naicko.
14. Doodroobal, ...	10	10	10	Ditto.
15. Thelibun, ...	40	40	40	Dhawara Bedha 40 Rupees,
16. Doodgarri, ruined.				
17. Kumplah, ditto.				
18. Kunplah, ditto.				
19. Wydhanee, ditto.				
20. Jugtikilla.				
21. Buldoor.				
22. Couriatoola.				

Byrades.			
Mootah, ...	25	15	25

Villages.	Houses.	Peons.	Ryots	Chiefs.
1. Teelisur, ...	15	15	10	Sahmo Padhano Gorotea.
2. Moosalo, ...	5	0	5	Jagurnaut Swamy.
3. Kootinaparra, ruined.				
4. Wyravosookopully, do.				
5. Bhamonogaum Ag^{m}. ...	10	0	10	Kolpol Bissye.
6. Boorboodee.				
7. Moosanpoory.				
8. Takoor.				

	Houses.	Peons.	Ryots.
The Fort of Poorna Cuttack, ...	85	26	59

And Villages.	Houses.	Peons.	Ryots.	Chiefs.
1. Cusba Poorna Cuttack ...	70	20	50	Tahkoroo Gorotea Dhowara Bedha 50 Rupees.
2. Proogdipalli, ruined.				
3. Salcottah, ditto.				

And Villages.	Houses.	Peons.	Ryots.	Chiefs.
4. Rajingy, ...	10	5	5	Ghassi Gorotea Dhowara Bedha 5 Rupees.
5. Boerah, ...	5	1	4	San Bissye ditto 4 Rupees.
6. Gracottah, ruined.				
7. Sookli.				
The Fort of Booerah,...	30	15	15	

Villages.	Houses.	Peons.	Ryots.	Chiefs.
1. Booerah Killah, ruined.				
2. Booerahgodo, ...	10	5	5	Mootho Gorotea.
3. Kontah, ruined.				
4. Hailloom, ditto.				
5. Bahmooshegodo, ditto.				
6. Thatrikillah, ...	20	10	10	Ditto.

THE THIRTEEN KHOND DISTRICTS IN BOAD.

1. Kotriekia included in the Khalisah.
2. Atcombo the 4 Eastern Combas.
3. Atcombo the 4 Eastern Combas or Ruttabarri.
4. Borogootza.
5. Bulscoopa.
6. Dommosinghi.
7. Oogdoor.
8. Bagjeer.
9. Baramullick.
10. Kolobogh.
11. Bondoghur.
12. Punchora or Baraboe Deo.
13. Saatmullick included in the Khalisah.

Khond Districts formerly attached to Boad now to Goomsur.

1. Chokapaud.
2. Hodzoghur.
3. Tenteliaghur.

Khond District attached to Duspullah.

1. Nowsagur.

Khond Districts of Boad.

1. Kotrikia.

Districts.	Chiefs.	Place of Residence.
Kotrikia.	Pattia Mullicko.	Kotrikia.

	Mootahs.	Villages.	Houses.	Peons.	Ryots.	Chiefs.
1.	Tulgaon, ...	......	......	......	......	Monna Khonro.
2.	Saatcun, ...	......	......	......	......	Pudlum Mullicko and Gungo Khonro.
3.	Oodgeejee,.........	Given under Boad, ...				Pertaul Mullicko Looklodo and Lutch Mullicko.
4.	Baramonda, ...	Mootah of Koossunghur,...				Khyra Junni, Khyra Khonro and Khya Mullicko.

EASTERN COMBOS OF ATCOMBO.

Chief Madhwa Khonro Raneegunze.

	Combos.	Chiefs.	Place of Residence.
1.	Adnygurra,..................	Niladri Khonro.	
2.	Teeleecoopah,..............	Munnoo Mullicko.	
3.	Korobin,......................	Ghassi ditto.	
4.	Contipudro, ...	Barunda ditto.	

1.	Adnygurra Combo,.........	124	17	0

	Villages.	Houses.	Peons.	Ryots.	Chiefs.
1.	Condrapadzo, ...	2	0	0	Mudwa Khonro.
2.	Dakpudra, ...	12	5	0	Gopanathoo Khonro.
3.	Gondapadzoo,...............	7	4	0	
4.	Kulgadoo, ...	9	0	0	Dona Majee.
5.	Moondeserum, ...	4	0	0	Goolah Jenni.
6.	Baringhee, ...	10	2	0	Sutti Naicko.
7.	Calniputty, ...	8	0	0	Soornye Khonro.
8.	Solaghur, ...	6	0	0	Dhoodhe Dehri.
9.	Cootzoopadzoo.				
10.	Oodoogoojy, ...	1	0	0	Dheenabundhoo Jenni.
11.	Raneeganze, ...	30	5	0	Madhwa Khonro.
12.	Soolagacur,..................	3	0	0	Oochooroo.
13.	Lingupadzoo.				
14.	Cooteehera,..................	8	0	0	Buttee Dhakoory.
15.	Gootzabany, ...	6	1	0	Badhua Mullicko.
16.	Barra ditto.				
17.	Soortagoonda, ...	3	0	0	Madhwa Khonro.
18.	Goodrisye, ...	8	0	0	Niladri Jenni.
19.	Coonda.				
20.	Coorada Kotah, ...	7	0	0	Dhigoo Bissye.
21.	Kojeri.				

Teeleecoopa, ...	17	8	0

	Villages.	Houses.	Peons.	Ryots.	Chiefs.
1.	Cusba Teebeecoopa, ...	10	6	0	Munno Mullicko.
2.	Baispurra.				
3.	Bakli.				
4.	Roaneepadah, ...	5	2	0	Borotho Padhano.
5.	Konoocottah, ...	2	0	0	Chotah Naicko.

	Houses.	Peons.	Ryots.
Korobui, ...	26	10	0

	Villages.	Houses.	Peons.	Ryots.	Chiefs.
1.	Cusba Korobui, ...	10	8	0	Ghassi Mullicko.
2.	Oripudro, ...	4	0	0	Mahnahjee Mulliko.
3.	Cootigno, ...	9	0	0	Ahdhi Mullicko.
4.	Pilsapudro, ...	3	2	0	Themma Pudhano.

	Houses.	Peons.	Ryots.
Contipudro Combo, ...	14	7	0

Villages.	Houses.	Peons.	Ryots.	Chiefs.
Cusba Contipudro, ...	8	6	0	Boorunda Mullicko.
Dadhipurra.				
Condra.				
Katspadzoo.				
Bundighur.				
Damooda, ...	3	1	0	Dhonia Bissye.
Dhongiamoonda, ...	3	0	0	Dhosye Chotah.

WESTERN COMBOS OF ATCOMBO OR RUTTABANY.

		Chiefs.	Place of Residence.
1.	Sooroodoocoopa, ...	Myser Mullicko.	
2.	Neerigoodee, ...	Batta Pudhano.	
3.	Turmeroo.		
4.	Madicola, ...	Murdo Ghutwal.	

1. Sooroodoocoopah.

	Villages.	Houses.	Peons.	Ryots.	Chiefs.
1.	Lindigoora.				
2.	Putinmena,..................	25	25	0	Bogwan Naicko.
3.	Koicompa.				
4.	Corno.				
5.	Jookroojee,..................	22	22	0	Nuttra Naicko.
6.	Janmenni, ...				Ditto.
7.	Borazora.				
8.	Moolikpurra, ...	20	20	0	Koopan Mullicko.
9.	Dootmendi, ...				Kondo ditto.

Villages.	Houses.	Peons.	Ryots.	Chiefs.
10. Tarmendi.				
11. Chelia,	1	1	0	Deroopi ditto.
12. Billabarri,	10	10	0	Sooben ditto.
13. Baricompa,	22	22	0	Deveha Pudhono.
14. Komarcole.				
15. Bahnibenni,	12	12	0	Rooshi Naicko.
16. Bahdigoodah,	11	11	0	Gorondo Mullicko.
17. Buddigoodah,	20	20	0	Soobem ditto.
18. Thadimory,	23	23	0	Doocha Pudhono.

BOROGOOTZA.

Dammo Jenni and Petta Dehri. Joint Chiefs of Borogootza.

It is divided into 3 Parris,	Chiefs.	Place of Residence.
1. Culliapuiri,	Dammo Jenni, Sansaroo Bakookoo and Nowbhun Mullicko,	The former lives in Orapadzo and the two latter in Bulliapara.
2. Delaparri,	Petta Dehri,	Charipurra.
3. Seerooparri,	Mudwa Singali Mullicko,	Kodjeripurra.

	Houses	Peons	Ryots	
Calliapuira,	155	150		

Villages.	Houses	Peons.	Ryots.	Chiefs.
1. Bulliapurra,	10	20	0	Nowbhum Mullicko, Sunsaroo Bakookoo.
2. Orapadzo,	10	5	0	Danmo Jenni.
3. Dohrigaun,	20	20	0	Jotia Mullicko.
4. Dhodahgaum,	20	20	0	Pedda Dehri.
5. Soratchuri,	20	20	0	Jogihi Mullicko.
6. Koolthasarri,	10	10	0	Madwa Barrico.
7. Boodawkallo,	5	5	0	Pedda Dehri.
8. Sorathola,	20	20	0	Kosta Mullicko.
9. Dorado,	20	20	0	Deera Mullicko.
10. Kirreedygoodah,	20	20	0	
Delaparri,	30	30	0	

Villages.	Houses.	Peons.	Ryots.	Chiefs.
1. Penamillia,	30	30	0	Sarungo Dehri.
2. Peepulparra,				Donrei Mulliko.
3. Charipurra,				Pella Dehri.
4. Serrocole,				Lubbo Mullicko.
5. Doomercole,				Gunza Ditto.
Seerooparri,				

	Villages.	Houses.	Peons.	Ryots.	Chiefs.
1.	Kodjeripurra, ...				Madwa Singali Mullicko.
2.	San Kodjirepur.				
3.	Oormoonda, ...				Ram Chunder Mullicko.
4.	Gonzapoora.				
5.	Eerpigoora.				
6.	Goonzapoorra.				
7.	Delapurry.				
8.	Kindygoora.				
9.	Pudhanpoora.				
10.	Sirambipoora.				
11.	Goonzilbunga.				
12.	Gondopudri.				
13.	Dainger Guttia Mullicko.				

BULSCOOPA DISTRICT.

Chiefs. Poorra Bissye.

	Mootahs.	Chiefs.	Place of Residence.
1.	Bengrikia, ...	Nagsun, Khonro Proohitchi Mal, ...	Lumbabaria Charapadzoo.
2.	Dootmendi, ...	Condo Matia Mullicko Kent Naicks, ...	Dootmendi.
3.	Grandimendi, ...	Dummo ditto, ...	Baricoopa.
4.	Bakomendi, ...	Pedro ditto, ...	Mullickpurra.
5.	Sangrimendi,............	Muno Padhano Dooloo Mul and Murcham, ...	Badisooka.
6.	Bupponmendi, ...	Sookri Mul, ...	Gidripadzoo.
7.	Rittoomendi, ...	Poonda Conro,...............	Boira.

Bengrikia Mootah.

	Villages.	Houses.	Peons.	Chiefs.
1.	Lumbabari, ...	30	30	Nagsun Khonro.
2.	Charapadzo, ...	8	8	Poosti Mullicko.
3.	Danzoo, ...	30	30	Jogithi ditto.
4.	Napakoopa, ...	9	9	Kasary ditto.
5.	Dolapara, ...	30	30	Dhoso ditto.
6.	Juppi, ...	25	25	Jomodhoro Khonro.
7.	Bondoli, ...	7	7	Nondhia Dehri.
8.	Noogaum,.........................	20	20	Neelah Naicko.
9.	Nogoledgi, ...	30	30	Dhandoo Mullicko.
10.	Goomaghur.			
11.	Seetalipooclra.			
	Kolingaun, ...	6	7	Bulloo Booyan.
	Zoogoodooputtoo, ...	20	20	Pratha Podhano.
	Kathapadhoo, ...	8	9	Sooboothi Jakaron.
	Budthooripadzoo,...............	2	2	Kalisa Khonro.
		225	227	

Dootmendi Mootah.

Raicole,	10	10	Mengoladhoro Mullicko.
Sidingi,	10	7	Ghassi Debri.
Koradacoopa,	8	10	Mahdwa Ditto.
Percoory,	5	18	Ditto Ditto.
Dootmendi,	40	30	Maha Mullicko.
Purnabarri,	5	5	Kthize Mullicko.
Bispurra,	30	30	Hoghodo Bissye.
Gonzoogoodah,	2	1	Ditto.
Goomagoodoo,	30	26	Podah Bissye.
Coradapurra.			
Magipurree.			
Khonripurree.			
Mullicksye.			
	140	137	

Grandimendi Mootah.

Jamjerry,	6	5	Gebajenni.
Dootpurra,	30	30	Jaidholo Khonro.
Berungpadzo.			
Sukkari,	7	6	Dhonro Debri.
Goodany,	8	10	Losejenni.
Patropudra,	30	6	Dhama Mullicko.
Barigootza,	4	4	Bikari Ditto.
Soodhooloogaun,	6	7	Markondah Jenni.
Koradookoompah,	5	5	Pirkoody Mullicko.
Pirkoody,	10	10	Kolady Debri.
Toolribunga,	10	10	Juckro Khonro.
Bactiagoodah,	3	3	Oozoole Mullicko.
Nuddeegoodah,	5	5	Moondelly Bavah.
	124	101	

Bakomendi Mootah.

Pudhemparra,	10	10	Deeree Podhono.
Pondrabary,	10	10	Bisoonoo Khonro.
Kittapadzo,			
Burrabui,			
Goondrybarry.			
Bidhoomendi,	10	10	Pettra Mullicko.
Bagamendi,	20	20	Ditto.
	50	50	

Sangrimendi Mootah.			
Barisooga,			
Dolpurra,	10	10	Morcha Khonro.
Goomagorro,			
Soodommendi,	8	8	Murtoo Ditto.
Golamendi,	6	6	Peringhi Ditto.
Kanrogora.			
Rachimendi,			
Konalli.			
Kennapadzo.			
Pundrimendi.			
Pisserpudro.			
	24	24	

Rupponmendi Mootah.			
Giridipadzo.			
Kabero.			
Lumbaketto.			
Surtacoolo,	5	5	Joojurry Mullicko.
Kodlimoonda,	10	10	Ditto.
Bulscoopa,	40	10	Poorah Bissye.
Pundrimendi,	5	5	Dhomono Khonro.
Jogodapoto,	10	10	Jogarry Mullicko.
Lungarikoompah,	10	10	Rajiboo ditto.
	80	50	

Rittoomendi Moodah.			
Bedoboe,	10	10	Dhodhia Mullicko.
Bagabendi,	10	10	Pettra ditto.
Thenapurra,	10	10	Ditto.
	30	30	

DOMMOSINGHI.

Chiefs.	*Place of Residence.*
Nitter Naieth Soodoo (Hindoo),	Polobadi.
Ghassi Mullicko Khond,	Terikia.
Bimia Mullicko,	Dokainghie.
Bassoo ditto,	Dokopal.

	Mootahs.	*Chiefs.*
1.	Koshiraboo,	Bassoo Mullicko.
2.	Terikia,	Ghassi.
3.	Dokainghee,	Binna.

Koohiraboo Mootah.	95	94

Villages.	*Houses.*	*Peons.*	*Ryots.*	*Chiefs.*
Cusba Koshiraboo, ...	40	40		Bassoo Mullicko.
Dammigami, ...	10	10		Isera Khonro.
Dakopal, ...	10	10		Bassoo Mullicko.
Soradagoora, ...	2	1		Sooderi Khonro.
Mojeribeda, ...	3	3		Ponica Mullicko.
Boodadun, ...	10	10		Goomeita Khonro.
Dooribarry, ...	20	20		Ranipah Mullicko.

Terikia, ...	59	59		

Villages.	*Houses.*	*Peons.*	*Ryots.*	*Chiefs.*
Cusba Terikia,............	40	40		Ghassi Mullicko.
Roojimgy, ...	10	40		Pahtha Khonro.
Koomoonapadah,.........	5	5		Dhondharye.
Mathavagonda, ...	1	1		Ghassi Mullicko.
Hooloowahinpurra, ...	3	3		Bahwa Juckoro.

Dokainghee Mootah,...	21	21		

Villages.	*Houses.*	*Peons.*	*Ryots.*	*Chiefs.*
Cusba Dokainghee, ...	3	3		Binna Mullicko.
Koondali, ...	10	10		Dhorobah Mullicko.
Gooteoopa, ...	4	4		Gundi Khonro.
Gorabundo, ...	4	4		

OOGDOOR.

Chiefs.		*Place of Residence.*
Babano Mullicko,..................................		Meniapadzo.
	100	

Villages.	*Houses.*	*Peons.*	*Ryots.*	*Chiefs.*
Muriapadzoo, ...	......	......	......	Babano Mullicko.
Mullickopurra, ...	......	......	......	Roopen Mullicko.
Booroobera, ...	......	......	......	Demsing.
Birgoor, ...	......	......	......	Moguli Gorotea.
Goorchall, ...	......	......	......	Bagona Mullicko.
Bolpurra, ...	......	......	......	Nundha ditto.
Frigripurra, ...	......	......	......	Bagra ditto.
Tootiunsing, ...	......	......	......	Donsinnoo.
Lohericottah, ...	......	......	......	Obi ditto.
Jogodolla, ...	......	......	......	Bika Mudhano.

BAGJEER.

Chiefs.	*Place of Residence.*
Goda Mullicko,	Isersirga.

140

Villages.	*Houses.*	*Peons.*	*Ryots.*	*Chiefs.*
Isersirga,	......	......	......	Goda Mullicko.
Koligaumy,	......	......	......	Bagro Jakore.
Buromal,	......	......	......	Sunsaw Mullicko.
Kondipara,	......	......	......	Kunjeel Jakore.
Komera.				
Boogtapurra,	......	......	......	Mooso Chotoga.
Barakoora,	......	......	......	Govind.
Gotzapurra.				
Nennen.				
Koorkoos,	......	......	......	Sirmeed Jenni.
Kotumsinghi,	......	......	......	Danno Pudhano.

KOLOBAGH.

Chiefs.

Durrai Mullicko Maja Mullicko, ... Sunnamy.
Pondi Khonro Hakem.
Sundolo Mullicko.

	Mootahs.	*Chiefs.*	*Place of Residence.*
1.	Gommamendi,	Rissa Mullock Songi Khonro.	
2.	Dappoomendi,	Tamuna Mullicko.	
3.	Olchamendi,	Kondera ditto.	

120

Villages.		*Peons.*		
Sunnamy,	......	......	......	Durrai Mullicko M. M.
Cotitora,	......	......	......	Rissa Mullicko.
Bellanpurra.				
Sodagam.				
Jamgee,	......	......	......	Pondi Khonro.
Peopulpura.				
Doomercole,	......	......	......	Tye Mullicko.
Poorunga,	......	......	......	Pondi Khonro, great man.
Komurcooda.				
Keermacote,	......	......	......	Naicks Mullicko or Boodi Mullicko.
Ketapadzoo,	......	......	......	Chundo Mullicko.

BONDOGHUR.

District.	*Chiefs.*	*Place of Residence.*
Bondoghur, ...	Bisskissan Bissye, ...	Peeringia.

Mootahs.	*Villages.*	*Houses.*	*Peons.*	*Ryots.*	*Chiefs.*
1. Sartingia.					
2. Moontingia.					

BARRAMULLICK.

Chiefs.	*Place of Residence.*
Bagwan Sow, ...	Bobera.
Madwa Sow.	
Mumi Sow.	
Nowbhun Sow, in honor of Khonds.	

100

Villages.

Bobera.
Komar.
Nuchina.
Boilpurra.
Dunbulos.
Toondapoora.
Koonagoongoo.
Toomgaum.
Bostumpoor.
Goondelia.
Loomboorjenna.
Penglaberra.
Barapoor.
Rautmal.
Nowapurra.
Joorcunoonda.
Kottoor.
Bundgaum.
Gunsunpurra.
Toonicumar.
Dalcumar.
Amjeer.
Tilpunga.

PUNCHORA.

Chief.—Rutto Mullicko, ... Punchora Barabae Des.

	Pergunnah,	*Villages.*	*Chiefs.*	*Place of Residence.*
1.	Punchora.			
2.	Punchpully,	12	Dimaroo Mullicko Jaukoor Dehri,	Moorpa.
3.	Kimmabeer,	15	Burmali Mullicko, Khond ditto,	Talpurra.
4.	Armool,	25	Mowkoon ditto, Bado ditto, ...	Burgaon.
5.	Bulundo,	25	Durto Khonro, a Jani,	Purra.
6.	Boogen,	25	Dytari ditto Dehri,	Rumghaut.
7.	Toorkia,	20	Kullyan Booi,	Manichpoor.
8.	Boobria,	25		
9.	Codrikia,	20	Joogsa Majee,	Gontapurra.
10.	Bamoor,	30	Sai Mullicko.	
11.	Petringia,	...	Hurry Bookta Muctiyar Jugbund Londo Mullicko,	Gootzapurra.
12.	Jellingia,	5	Hurry Bookla.	
13.	Surmoonda,	20	Korkita Mullicko,	Sogoda.

SAATMULLICK.

Chiefs.	*Place of Residence.*
Boobini Mullicko,	Bolinda.

80

Villages.	*Houses.*	*Peons.*	*Ryots.*	
Bolinda,	......	......	......	Boobini Mullicko.
Badicota.				
Sapora,	......	......	......	Onto Majee.
Kodjupudro,	......	......	......	Boode Jakore.
Moncamor.				
Chelibali.				
Bausini.				
Hillany in Borades.				
Contatricola.				
Halwalatricole,	......	......	......	Hotwa Pudhano.
Dongerageer.				
Tentulepulli.				
Poorcall.				
Tainjun.				

HODGOGHORO.

KABO MULLICKO, KHOND CHIEFS.

Hindu Chiefs, San Bissye Pooranaghur.

Mootahs.	*Chiefs.*	*Place of Residence.*
Sakringia,	Poorooha Mullicko,	Peetera.
Moorungia,	Bolomo Ditto,	Moorungia.

Mootahs.	*Chiefs.*	*Place of Residence.*
Ramgia,	Sarungarai,	Roothamendi.
Booringia,	Bagri Mullicko,	Dolpurra.
Boojulmendi,	Roopia Ditto.	
Bopulmendi,	Dadi Ditto,	Beerigaum.

Sakringia Mootah.
Moorungia Ditto.

	Villages.	*Houses.*	*Peons.*	*Chiefs.*
1.	Cusba Peetera,	5	5	Poorooha Mullicko.
2.	Oopercoloo,	20	20	Mungilah Khnro.
3.	Neelorogaun,	8	8	Gombiro ditto.
4.	Pillikigaum,	15	15	Gosoo ditto.
5.	Kinidicottah,	5	5	Ditto ditto.
6.	Moorungia Cusba,	10	10	Bolomo Mullicko.
7.	Podhonogaun,	20	20	Byah Khonro.
8.	Dhoodigaun,	20	20	Keddha Mullicko.
9.	Thalarimah,	10	10	Antoo Khonro.
10.	Jabidi,	10	10	Ditto ditto.
11.	Kassirikolloo,	8	8	Poorah Mullicko.
12.	Ridahsinghi,	10	10	Dyssi ditto.
13.	Dussagoora.			
14.	Teenicondoo.			

Ramgia Mootah.
Booringiah Mootah.

Villages.	*Houses.*	*Peons.*	*Chiefs.*
Cushba Pooranaghur,	40	40	San Bissoye.
Roothamendi,	50	50	Sarungarai.
Solopogum,	40	40	Boddah Pudhano.
Gyrigaum,	20	20	Donnuma Khonro.
Boodingia,	60	60	Dhussurrah Mullicko.
Ryingia,	30	30	Pahbira ditto.
Topadingia,	80	80	Gonat Kolah.
Sonkurrakolo,	100	100	Rutte Khonro.
Kudjoogaun,	40	40	Monye ditto.
Ponasogoodah,	15	15	Ditto.
Neddeegoodah,	5	5	Ditto.
Jenagaum,	120	120	Majee Khonro.
Gondagaun,	100	100	Robi ditto.
Badrigoodah,	40	40	Badri Mullicko.
Boojarimendi,	30	30	Joojahri ditto.
Voodapurra,	10	10	Boh ditto.
Poahrogaun,	10	10	Gahi ditto.

Villages.	*Houses.*	*Peons.*	*Chiefs.*
Rathioacoloo,	20	20	Chemnieli ditto.
Kutthimendi,	10	10	Ruddi Khonro.
Kundapurra,	20	20	Prajoo ditto.
Cooragaroo.			
Pooroohahis.			
Dulpurra Cusba,	......	......	Bagri Mullicko.
Chedhyahdoo,	10	10	Madhoo Bissye.

Boojulmendi Mootah.
Bopulmendi ditto.

Villages.	*Houses.*	*Peons.*	*Chiefs.*
Bopulmendi Cusba,	40	40	Dadi Mullicko.
Thenthaligaun,	6	6	Jundahroopo.
Sheelookabondhoo,	10	10	Dadi Mullicko.

TENTELIAGHUR.

Khond Chief Rabo Mullicko Ootansing Dolabera.

	Mootahs.	*Chiefs.*	*Place of Residence.*
1.	Suckadingia,	Erubli Mullicko,	Suckadingia.
2.	Tenteliaghur,	Ootansing,	Tenteliaghur.
3.	Sonapungia,	Wanasha Pradhanum,	Soonapungia.
4.	Tomusmendi,	Ungily Pudhano,	Goodrigah.
5.	Bapoonamendi,	Pooso Pudhano,	Bapoonamendi.
6.	Komaragaun,	Somye Khonro,	Kummogoodah.

Suckadingia Mootah,	10	12	
Cusba Suckadingia,	10	12	Erubli Mullicko.
Tenteliaghur Mootah,	181	102	

		Houses.	*Peons.*	*Chiefs.*
1.	Cusba Tenteliaghur,	40	30	Ootan Sing.
2.	Bostingia,	10	5	Dainga Mullicko.
3.	Suthorogaun,	15	10	Nobo Khonro.
4.	Kumbagoodah,	4	2	Kundra Pudhano.
5.	Moonishigaun,	10	5	Ahmilah Khonro.
6.	Godriga,	10	5	Boodra Ditto.
7.	Morrisogoodah,	4	2	Roopo Ditto.
8.	Thorohpoottoo,	5	2	Dhobana Ditto.
9.	Potacuttuck,	20	10	Peroo Mullicko
10.	Billagodo,	15	5	Bidho Khonro.

	Houses.	Peons.	Chiefs.
11. Kodjeripurra, ...	10	5	Eruppoo Ditto.
12. Roongoo, ...	8	4	Roongoo Ditto.
13. Tonkolomendi, ...	10	5	Nondho Ditto.
14. Borogaum, ...	10	5	Soonah Ditto.
15. Paringia, ...	10	7	Rabo Mullicko.

Soonapungia Mootah, ...	...	...

Villages.	Houses.	Peons.	Chiefs.
1. Cusba Soonapungia, ...	......	......	Woorasha Pradhanum.
2. Bochooroo Padah, ...	......	......	Bochooroo ditto.
3. Bellirimendi, ...	......	......	Govindhoo Mullicko.
4. Koosoomendi, ...	......	......	Budah Juckaro.

Tomusmendi Mootah, ...	59	59

Villages.	Houses.	Peons.	Chiefs.
1. Goodrigah, ...	10	10	Ungily Pudhano.
2. Vondeegoodah, ...	8	8	Dhissera Mullicko.
3. Dongeripadah, ...	7	7	Sobono ditto.
4. Shimalli, ...	6	6	Domuno ditto.
5. Dholoopara, ...	20	20	Bootah ditto.
6. Goodah Koompah, ...	8	8	Poricha ditto
7. Moondagaum, ruined.			

Bapoonamendi Mootah, ...	53	49

Villages.	Houses.	Peons.	Chiefs.
1. Cusba Bapoonamendi, ...	20	20	Pooso Pudhano.
2. Punnabadi, ...	15	15	Jnji Mullicko.
3. Solagoodah, ...	10	10	Bickrama Mullicko.
4. Daloopongah, ...	8	4	Pooso Pudhano.

Komaragaun Mootah, ...	73	64

Villages.	Houses.	Peons.	Chiefs.
1. Kummagoodah, ...	6	5	Somye Khonro.
2. Thundigoodah, ...	10	6	Juganah ditto.
3. Thokomg, ...	20	20	Kosha ditto.
4. Thethicaponga, ...	8	7	Duggeri Juckoro.
5. Poornapany, ...	7	6	Pithae Khonro.
6. Ponspodhro, ...	12	10	Noyono Tholabara.
7. Moonthemy, ...	10	10	Kimpa Khonro.

CHOKAPAUD.

Soodoo Chief Ragnat Bissye, ... Chokapaud.
Khond Chief Baghera Mullicko.

	Mootahs.	*Chiefs.*	*Place of Residence.*
1.	Coondaputro, ...	Nunda Mullicko,...	Nilligooda.
2.	Lackrikia, ...	Wobine ditto, ...	Lackrikia Goodrisye.
3.	Cotringia, ...	Hudera ditto, ...	Jaudpore.
4.	Wurchingi, ...	Oojooloo ditto, ...	Wurchingi.
5.	Noondini, ...	Borodi ditto, ...	Chumputty Rae.
6.	Godingia, ...	Narrapah Pudhano,	Boroli.
7.	Metringia, ...	Daboo Mullicko,...	Boodagheitti.
8.	Chokapaud, ...	Rugnat Bissye, ...	Chokapaud.
9.	Posera, ...	Purma ditto, ...	Posera.
10.	Ulingia, ...	Seetalo Mullicko,	Kisticolo.
11.	Dolicompa, ...	Bagera ditto, ...	Dungagaum.
12.	Kama, ...	Dhomano ditto, ...	Bodopurra.

Coondaputro Mootah, ... 182

	Villages.	*Houses.*	*Chiefs.*
1.	Cusba Nelligooda, ...	21	Nunda Mullicko.
2.	Talagotza, ...	6	Bono Coniero.
3.	Codicado,.............................	10	Gonno Khonro.
4.	Dainghee, ...	8	Taiya Mullicko.
5.	Pooroogadya, ...	5	Jooja Khonro.
6.	Gattigooda, ...	20	Buckshe Mullicko.
7.	Dolicko, ...	7	Kundera ditto.
8.	Barabully, ...	8	
9.	Joorookang, ruined,.................	...	Ujar.
10.	Boorapudo, ...	10	Joojo Mullicko.
11.	Deegee, ...	11	
12.	Onoragada, ...	12	Bagree Mullicko.
13.	Gonjegoora, ...	11	
14.	Midjagado, ...	13	Biree ditto.
15.	Ningremoonda, ...	12	
16.	Kooradungee, ...	14	Bagree ditto.
17.	Leeagodo, ...	5	Ditto.
18.	Peepulapudro,.......................	4	Ditto.
19.	Billisye, ...	3	Paduca ditto.
20.	Booroomoonda, ...	...	Ujar.
21.	Dulima, ...	2	Dootea ditto.
	Lackrikia Mootah,.................	25	

	Villages.	Houses.	Chiefs.
1.	Cusba Lackrikia Goodrisye, ...	6	Wobino Mullicko.
2.	Thorosye, ...	2	
3.	Jarikereddy,........................	3	Pudhano ditto.
4.	Punropudro, ...	4	Zenda ditto.
5.	Packutchera, ...	6	Oogly ditto.
6.	Teelubadee,........................	4	Roosoo Pradhano.

Cotringia Mootah, ... 36

	Villages.	Houses.	Chiefs.
1.	Cusba Jondpore, ...	16	Andera Mullicko.
2.	Dongagaumy, ...	3	Bagrie ditto.
3.	Soobooliah, ...	4	Towree Pradhano.
4.	Muttapunhalo,........................	5	Ratnudea Eerie.
5.	Behragoda, ...	3	Huddu Pradhano.
6.	Sodapudra, ...	6	Bondo ditto.
7.	Tottagooda,........................	7	Nuddee Khonro.
8.	Tangiri, ...	9	Zilla ditto.
9.	Peepulopudro, ...	10	Kooloosamro.
10.	Coombarikhani, ...	11	Jooja Mullicko.
11.	Gerody, ...	4	Ujooloo Khonro.
12.	Hattibaree, ...	2	Borisokomna.
13.	Rindibarree, ...	4	Sitila Khonro.
14.	Borodakoloo, ...	2	

Wurchungi Mootah, ... 20

	Villages.	Houses.	Chiefs.
1.	Cusba Wurchungi, ...	10	Oojoolo Mullicko.
2.	Dakalabadi, ...	2	Soodda ditto.
3.	Moojesye, ...	3	
4.	Warchingi, ...	5	Nichela Khonro.

Noondini Mootah, ... 36

	Villages.	Houses.	Chiefs.
1.	Cusba Chumputty Rae,............	14	Borodi Mullicko.
2.	Barapall, ...	3	Sunga ditto.
3.	Mootoopunkaloo, ...	2	
4.	Noorisye,........................	5	Moori ditto.
5.	Pokalakia, ...	5	
6.	Chumputty Rae,....................	5	

Godingia Mootah, ... 27

	Villages.	*Houses.*	*Chiefs.*
1.	Cusba Boroli, ...	15	Narrapah Pudhano.
2.	Seeroomoogaum, ...	1	Dhamono Mullicko.
3.	Delingia, ...	3	Mootoojunhera.
4.	Gestikoloo, ...	4	Sitila Mullicko and Gonno Mullicko.
5.	Rongomuttia, ...	4	Deddi Mullicko.

Metringia Mootah, ... 38

	Villages.	*Houses.*	*Chiefs.*
1.	Cusba Boodaghatti, ...	16	Duboo Mullicko.
2.	Jittaghatti, ...	4	Dun Mullicko.
3.	Puddooma, ...	5	Lora Pradhano.
4.	Oodra, ...	3	
5.	Debingia, ...	10	Dommera Mullicko.

Chokapaud Mootah, ... 66

	Villages.	*Houses.*	*Chiefs.*
1.	Cusba Chokapaud, ...	6	Rugnal Bissye.
2.	Chokapaud, ...	29	Ditto.
3.	Gonkapudra, ...	4	Ditto.
4.	Pundreseema, ...	10	Binodo Naicko.
5.	Bahmuno Padro, ...	10	San Bissye.
6.	Coirasye, ...	2	Corrpa Naickoo.
7.	Bodookacollo, ...	5	Ghassi Pradhano.
8.	Tholomoondolu, ...	0	Soornoona Mullicko.

Posera Mootah, ... 65

	Villages.	*Houses.*	*Chiefs.*
1.	Cuba Posera, ...	8	Purma Bissye.
2.	Posera, ...	30	
3.	Tindasye, ...	5	Jettiadosoo Pudhano.
4.	Borodygodo, ...	8	Sunga Mullicko.
5.	Kumdodo, ...	4	Dagoo ditto.
6.	Napanea, ...	4	Cundra ditto.
7.	Ronagam, ...		Ujar.
8.	Brodrikia, ...	8	Junga Mullicko.
9.	Chaly, ...	...	Bisikissinna Bissye.

Ulingia Mootah, ... 12

	Villages.	Houses.	Chiefs.
1.	Cusba Kisticolo, ...	4	Seetola Mullicko.
2.	Pajeedonga, ...	4	Borjee ditto.
3.	Bummeragaoi, ...	4	Rain ditto.
4.	Binzeroogaum, ...		Binzoo ditto.

Dolicomga Mootah near Chala,...

	Villages.			
1.	Cusba, ...			
2.	Moothooponkalo, ...	10	5	Pudhano.
3.	Pocallica, ...	6	2	Ditto.
4.	Sompathirge, ...	1	0	Rye Naicko.

NOWSAGUR.

	Mootahs.	Chiefs.	Place of Residence.
1.	Nowsagur, ...	Osera Majee, ...	Booroopal.
2.	Sattopully, ...	Jilodora Janna, ...	Korodacoompa.
3.	Jennadas, ...	Poorsotto Mahalicko, ...	Gooragaum.
4.	Tolocumbo, ...	Otzoto Majee, ...	Perupurra.

Nowsagur Mootah,... 149 129 171 30

	Villages.	Houses.	Peons.	Wet cultivation in Burnus.	Dry cultivation in Burnus.	Chiefs.
1.	Cusba Booroopalla, ...	20	15	15	5	Osera Majee.
2.	Moondela, ...	4	4	20	5	Labra Mullicko.
3.	Bonee,.................	5	3	30	10	Osera Majee.
4.	Koombekeela,.........	5	5	8	3	Koolisingi Janni.
5.	Dosundiporee, ...	4	4	20	5	Tangona Janni.
6.	Bandelagatza,.........	4	4	2	0	Krya Khonro.
7.	Nibbagutza, ...	3	3	2	0	Gadie Mullicko.
8.	Konkonomundy,......	8	10	10	2	Dhamona ditto.
9.	Naichagaum, ...	4 tordoo.	4	3	0	Beemo Naick.
10.	Nipari, ...	7	8	4	0	Rajo Majee.
11.	Goondribara, ...	2	2	2	0	Kukalo Pudhano.
12.	Patroogaon, ...	2	2	1	0	Jogserohe.
13.	Siviseera, ...	7	5	4	0	Cartika Dehri.
14.	Koradungi, ...	2	3	2	0	Boondia Dehri.
15.	Jorekibari, ...	15	15	15	0	Madwa Khonro.
16.	Doora,.................	8	6	15	0	Ditto.
17.	Tolapadzoo, ...	5	6	5	0	Tittoo Janni.
18.	Koneroo,..............	4	2	3	0	Onkoro Janni.
19.	Sodapudro, ...	4	3	1	0	Gundero Mullicko.
20.	Garriapurra, ...	12	10	4	0	Dundia ditto.
21.	Koonnicolo, ...	15	10	4	0	Rusba Khonro.
22.	Jeevanogondah, ...	5	5	1	0	Toonta Mullicko.
	Sattopully Mootah,...	41	53	50	22	

	Villages.	*Houses.*	*Peons.*	*Wet Culti-vation.*	*Dry Culti-vation.*	*Chiefs.*
1.	Cusba Korodacoompa	15	20	10	10	Jolodera Janni.
2.	Baneegotza, ...	12	12	15	5	Mohona Bogotee.
3.	Pullapadzo,............	4	4	3	3	Rutto Khonro.
4.	Tankoora, ...	8	15	20	4	Batti Pradhano.
5.	Gorosagaon, ...	2	2	2	0	Jolodora Janni.
	Jennadas Mootah, ...	62	79	57	11	

	Villages.	*Houses.*	*Peons.*	*Wet Culti-vation.*	*Dry Culti-vation.*	*Chiefs Property in.*
1.	Cusba Gooragaum,...	10	20	15	5	Poorsotto Mullicko Gooragaum, ... 20
2.	Banebeeri, ...	5	3	2	0	Gooma Ditto Gotzabam, 2
3.	Dorikipadzo, ...	8	8	4	0	Bootika Janni Gootibuny, 3
4.	Goondribari, ...	3	4	2	5	Bola Ditto Koomrookola, 2
5.	Tungaleeri,............	3	4	2	1	Bikummo Mullicko.
6.	Asadagaum, ...	5	5	4	0	Conto Majee.
7.	Punnawari,............	5	5	4	0	
8.	Dikri,...................	5	5	4	0	Kobsi Janni.
9.	Baejerri,...............	10	15	13	0	Coira Khonro.
10.	Gotzabari, ...	4	4	2	0	Poorsotto Mahalicko.
11.	Cootibarri, ...	1	2	3	0	
12.	Koomrookolo,.........	3	4	2	0	
	Tolocumbo Mootah, .	21	25	6	1	

	Villages.	*Houses.*	*Peons.*	*Wet Culti-vation.*	*Dry Culti-vation.*	*Chiefs Property in.*
1.	Cusba Pempurra, ...	10	12	0	0	Otzoto Majee Pemparra, ... 20 5
2.	Mundoli,........	3	3	1	0	Konnora Janni.
3.	Meelisora, ...	8	10	5	1	Sookoolo Ditto.
4.	Gondisora, ...	0	0	0	0	Rajah has taken.

(Signed) S. C. MACPHERSON, *Lieut. A. Surveyor General.*

Madras, 21st June, 1841.

(A true copy,)

Hy. CHAMIER, *Chief Secretary.*

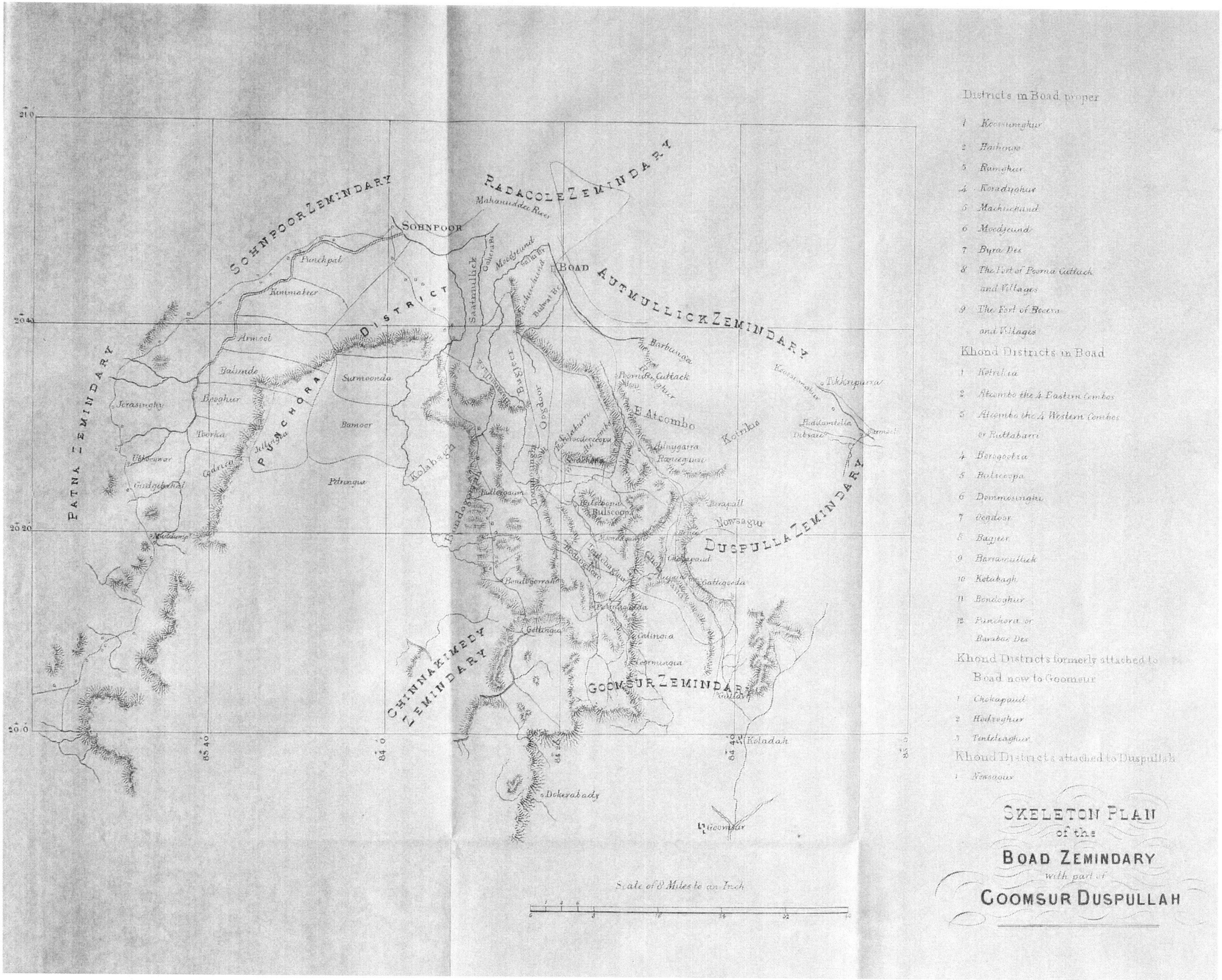

SKELETON PLAN
of the
BOAD ZEMINDARY
with part of
GOOMSUR DUSPULLAH
Districts in Boad proper
1 Koosumghur
2 Bashonga
3 Rumghur
4 Koradyghur
5 Machuchand
6 Moodjeund
7 Byra Des
8 The Fort of Poorna Cuttack and Villages
9 The Fort of Beera and Villages
Khond Districts in Boad
1 Kotrikia
2 Atcombo the 4 Eastern Combos
3 Atcombo the 4 Western Combos or Ruttabarri
4 Borogootra
5 Bulscoopa
6 Dommosinghi
7 Oogdoor
8 Bagjeer
9 Barramullick
10 Kotabagh
11 Bondoghur
12 Punchora or Barabar Des
Khond Districts formerly attached to Boad now to Goomsur
1 Chokapaud
2 Hodzoghur
3 Tentelaghur
Khond Districts attached to Duspullah
1 Nowsagur
SOHNPOOR ZEMINDARY
RADACOLE ZEMINDARY
AUTMULLICK ZEMINDARY
DUSPULLA ZEMINDARY
GOOMSUR ZEMINDARY
CHINNAKIMEDY ZEMINDARY
PATNA ZEMINDARY
DISTRICT
PUNCHORA
SOHNPOOR
BOAD
Mahanuddee River
E Atcombo
Kotrikia
Nowsagur
Koladah
Goomsur
Dokerabady
Scale of 8 Miles to an Inch